聽說讀打寫

Textbook
(Traditional Character Edition)

羅秋昭　　薛意梅
Julie LO　　Emily YIH

CENGAGE
Learning®

Andover • Melbourne • Mexico City • Stamford, CT • Toronto • Hong Kong • New Delhi • Seoul • Singapore • Tokyo

Go! Chinese Go300 Textbook
(Traditional Character Edition)

Julie Lo, Emily Yih

Publishing Director:
Roy Lee

Editorial Manager, CLT:
Lan Zhao

Development Editor:
Coco Koh

Associate Development Editor:
Titus Teo

Senior Product Manager (Asia):
Joyce Tan

Product Manager (Outside Asia):
Mei Yun Loh

Creative Manager:
Melvin Chong

Regional Manager, Production & Rights:
Pauline Lim

Production Executive:
Evan Wu

For product information and technology assistance, contact us at
Cengage Learning Asia Customer Support, 65-6410-1200

For permission to use material from this text or product,
submit all requests online at **www.cengageasia.com/permissions**
Further permission questions can be emailed to
asia.permissionrequest@cengage.com

ISBN-13: 978-981-4281-47-8
ISBN-10: 981-4281-47-6

Cengage Learning Asia Pte Ltd
151 Lorong Chuan
#02-08 New Tech Park
Singapore 556741

Cengage Learning is a leading provider of customized learning solutions with office locations around the globe, including Andover, Melbourne, Mexico City, Stamford (CT), Toronto, Hong Kong, New Delhi, Seoul, Singapore, and Tokyo. Locate your local office at
www.cengage.com/global

Cengage Learning products are represented in Canada by Nelson Education, Ltd.

For product information, visit **www.cengageasia.com**

Photo credits
(Below photo-numbers only © 2010 Jupiterimages Corporation)
Cover: © Charly Franklin/Taxi/Getty Images; AB20576. p. 7: 9394436; p. 11: 8801902; p. 12: 11764494; p. 16: (top to bottom, left to right) © iStockphoto.com/David Cerven; 4425081; 4932267; 12596659; 3659394; © Barry Austin/Digital Vision/Getty Images; 200403808-001; © iStockphoto.com/Andrew Rich; 7179004; 11970177; © Nicole Hill/Rubber Ball Productions/ Getty Images; 83606627; 11851970; p. 24: (top to bottom) 10977289; 9005321; 13164971; 12191536; p. 28: (top to bottom, left to right) 5251343; iStockphoto.com; 8266133; 11948058; © Photos.com; 11948008; iStockphoto.com/Chris Schmidt; 4677373; 9115213; p. 36: (top to bottom) 11833570; 9211299; p. 37: © iStockphoto.com; 884966; p. 40: (top to bottom, left to right) © iStockphoto.com/Guillermo Perales; 7694342; © iStockphoto.com/Arpad Nagy-Bagoly; 8674036; © iStockphoto.com/John McLaird; 8509270; © iStockphoto.com/Thomas Perkins; 5329238; © iStockphoto.com/Jason Lugo; 4725348; © iStockphoto.com/Dean Turner; 7474342; © iStockphoto.com/Aldo Murillo; 6494884; © iStockphoto.com/Catherine Yeulet; 7639733; © iStockphoto/Tomas Bercic; 9246918; © iStockphoto.com/Joey Nelson; 5194661; p. 44: 13157629; p. 49: (top to bottom) 13133624; 13226574; Goh Siok Hian/Dreamstime.com; 8310273; p. 50: © iStockphoto.com; 9559099; p. 61: 12762273; p. 64: (top to bottom, left to right) 3906631; 3187019; 6299043; 4926808; 11943729; 10792758; 12837931; 12569484; p. 72: (top to bottom) 5084162; 8927640; 3662299; 3186161; p. 76: (top to bottom, left to right) 4533220; 4822235; 2723433; 13108506; 5804642; 9059522; © iStockphoto.com; 1161367; © iStockphoto.com/Elianet Ortiz; 458660; p. 88: iStockphoto.com/Daniel Loiselle; 5566718; p. 88: (top to bottom, left to right) 6301621; 4982693; 5012408; 3184739; 13010198; © iStockphoto.com/Yenwen Lu; 5169858; 4824738; 4524920; 3645143; p. 96: (top to bottom) 7443138; 5267758; 6300844; 12296097; p. 108: 12282103; p. 112: (top to bottom, left to right) © iStockphoto.com/Ed Wilde; 2972259; 12275086; 10569177; 9425994; 5330850; 9191277; 13228313; 5259505; 5331303; 4857477; p. 113: (top to bottom) 5067759; 9082010; 2699530.

Printed in Taiwan
11 12 13 16 15 14

Acknowledgements

Go! Chinese is designed to be used together with *IQChinese Go* courseware, a series of multimedia CD-ROM developed by **IQChinese**. We sincerely thank **Wu, Meng-Tien** (Instruction Manager, IQChinese) and **Lanni Wang** (Instruction Specialist, IQChinese) for their tremendous editorial support and advice throughout the development of this program.

We also like to thank the following individuals who offered many helpful insights, ideas, and suggestions for improvement during the product development stage of *Go! Chinese*.

- **Jessie Lin Brown**, Singapore American School, Singapore
- **Henny Chen**, Moreau Catholic High School, USA
- **Yeafen Chen**, University of Wisconsin-Milwaukee, USA
- **Christina Hsu**, Superior Education, USA
- **Yi Liang Jiang**, Beijing Language and Culture University, China
- **Yan Jin**, Singapore American School, Singapore
- **Kerman Kwan**, Irvine Chinese School, USA
- **Chi-Chien Lu**, IBPS Chinese School, USA
- **Andrew Scrimgeour**, University of South Australia, Australia
- **James L. Tan**, Grace Christian High School, the Philippines
- **Man Tao**, Koning Williem I College, the Netherlands
- **Chiungwen Tsai**, Westside Chinese School, USA
- **Tina Wu**, Westside High School, USA
- **YaWen (Alison) Yang**, Concordian International School, Thailand

Preface

Go! Chinese, together with **IQChinese Go** multimedia **CD-ROM**, is a fully-integrated Chinese language program that offers an easy, enjoyable, and effective learning experience for learners of Chinese as a foreign language.

The themes and lesson plans of this program are designed with references to the American National Standards for Foreign Language Learning developed by ACTFL[1], and the Curriculum Guides for Modern Languages developed by the Toronto District Board of Education. The program aims to help beginners develop their communicative competence in the four language skills of listening, speaking, reading, and writing while gaining an appreciation of the Chinese culture, exercising their ability to compare and contrast different cultures, making connections with other discipline areas, and extending their learning experiences to their homes and communities.

The program employs innovative teaching methodologies and computer applications to enhance language learning, as well as keep students motivated in and outside of the classroom. The companion CD-ROM gives students access to audio, visual, and textual information about the language all at once. Chinese typing is systematically integrated into the program to facilitate the acquisition and retention of new vocabulary and to equip students with a skill that is becoming increasingly important in the Internet era wherein more and more professional and personal correspondence are done electronically.

Course Design

The program is divided into two series: Beginner and Intermediate. The Beginner Series, which comprises four levels (Go100-400), provides a solid foundation for continued study of the Intermediate Series (Go500-800). Each level includes a student text, a workbook, and a companion CD-ROM.

Beginner Series: Go100 – Go400

Designed for zero beginners, each level of the Beginner Series is made up of 10 colorfully illustrated lessons. Each lesson covers new vocabulary and simple sentence structures with particular emphasis on listening and speaking skills. In keeping with the communicative approach, a good mix of activities such as role play, interviews, games, pair work, and language exchanges are incorporated to allow students to learn to communicate through interaction in the target language. The CD-ROM uses rhythmic chants, word games, quizzes, and Chinese typing exercises to improve students' pronunciation, mastery of *pinyin*, and their ability to recognize and read words and sentences taught in each lesson.

The Beginner Series can be completed in roughly 240 hours (160 hours on Textbook and 80 hours on CD-ROM). Upon completion of the Beginner Series, the student will have acquired approximately 500 Chinese characters and 1000 common phrases.

Intermediate Series: Go500 – Go800

The Intermediate Series continues with the use of the communicative approach, but places a greater emphasis on Culture, Community, and Comparison. Through stories revolving around Chinese-American families, students learn vocabulary necessary for expressing themselves in a variety of contexts, describing their world, and discussing cultural differences.

The Intermediate Series can be completed in roughly 320 hours (240 hours on Textbook and 80 hours on CD-ROM). Upon completion of both the Beginner and Intermediate Series, the student will have acquired approximately 1000 Chinese characters and 2400 common phrases.

---

[1] American Council on the Teaching of Foreign Languages (http://www.actfl.org)

Vocabulary and Sentence Structures

The program places emphasis on helping students use the target language in contexts relevant to their everyday lives. Therefore, the chosen vocabulary and sentence structures are based on familiar topics such as family, school activities, hobbies, weather, shopping, food, pets, modes of transport, etc. The same topics are revisited throughout the series to reinforce learning, as well as to expand on the vocabulary and sentence structures acquired before.

Listening and Speaking

Communicative activities encourage and require a learner to speak with and listen to other learners. Well-designed and well-executed communicative activities can help turn the language classroom into an active and enjoyable place where learners are motivated to learn and can learn what they need. The program integrates a variety of communicative activities such as role play, interviews, games, pair work, and language exchanges to give students the opportunity to put what they have learned into practice.

Word Recognition and Reading

Each lesson introduces about 12 new Chinese characters. Using the spiral approach, each new character is first introduced and then recycled in classroom activities and subsequent lessons to enhance retention of new vocabulary over time. *Pinyin* (phonetic notation) is added above newly introduced characters so that students can learn to pronounce them. To make sure students do not become over-reliant on *pinyin* to read Chinese, recycled vocabulary is stripped of *pinyin* so that students can learn to recognize and read the actual written characters in due course. For the same reason, the companion CD-ROM does not display the *pinyin* of words automatically.

Type-to-Learn Methodology

The unique characteristic of this series is the use of Chinese typing as an instructional strategy to improve listening, pronunciation, and word recognition. Activities in the CD-ROM require students to type characters or sentences as they are read aloud or displayed on the computer screen. Students will be alerted if they make a mistake and will be given the chance to correct them. If they do not get it right on the third try, the software provides immediate feedback on how to correct the error. This interactive trial-and-error process allows students to develop self-confidence and learn the language by doing.

TYPE Chinese characters with the 26 letters of the alphabet

HEAR Chinese words read aloud

SEE the correct Chinese character

USE multiple senses to learn

Chinese Characters and Character Writing

The program does not require the student to be able to hand-write all the core vocabulary; the teacher may however assign more character writing practice according to his or her classroom emphasis and needs. What the program aims to do is to give students a good grasp of Chinese radicals and stroke order rules, as well as to help students understand and appreciate the characteristics and formation of Chinese characters. The program includes writing practice on frequently used characters. Understanding the semantic function radicals have in the characters they form and having the ability to see compound characters by their simpler constituents enable students to memorize new characters in a logical way.

Using the CD-ROM as an Instructional Aid

The following diagram shows how a teacher might use the CD-ROM as an instructional aid to improve traditional classroom instruction.

Textbook | **Multimedia CD-ROM**

Segment 1
(1st class hour)

WARM-UP
Arouse students' interest and set the tone for the whole lesson

Get Started—Additional topic-related words to expand students' vocabulary for daily conversation

Segment 2
(2nd class hour)

Let's CHANT
Rhyming text to be read aloud

Segment 3
(3rd class hour)

 ### Let's Learn GRAMMAR
Grammar

Segment 4
(4th class hour)

Let's TALK

Scripted dialogue practice that may be extended or modified

Let's Learn CHARACTER   ### Let's Learn RADICAL   ### Let's Learn PUNCTUATION

Learn about Chinese characters, radicals, and punctuation

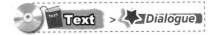

Segment 5
(5th class hour)

Let's READ

Reading and comprehension

Let's DO IT

Review and reinforcement activities

Segment 6
(6th class hour)

LEARNING LOG
Conclusion and students' self-evaluation

#Sentence Quiz Exercise

The section *Exercise > Sentence Quiz* in the CD-ROM enhances learning by stimulating multiple senses as well as providing immediate feedback on students' performance.

The Sentence Quiz exercise comprises four levels.

- Level 1 – Warm-up Quiz (Look, Listen, and Type): Chinese text, *pinyin*, and audio prompts are provided.

- Level 2 – Visual-aid Quiz: Only Chinese text is provided. There are no *pinyin* or audio prompts.

- Level 3 – Audio-aid Quiz: Only audio prompts are provided.

- Level 4 – Character-selection Quiz: Only Chinese text is provided. After entering the correct *pinyin*, students are required to select the correct character from a list of similar-looking characters.

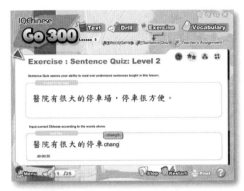

Typing practice for important sentences in every lesson reinforces the connection between words and sounds, and helps students to identify words better.

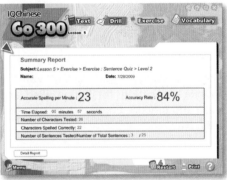

Summary Report immediately reveals students' accuracy rate and speed of typing per minute.

Detail Report lists characters typed erroneously three times during the quiz. It also shows details of errors based on categories such as *pinyin*, tone, and word selection. The instant feedback feature enables students to start on self-improvement right away.

Classroom Setup and Equipment

For small classes (up to 5 students), the teacher can show the CD-ROM features on one computer with students gathered around the screen. For large groups, a projector will be needed to project the computer's display onto a large screen so that the entire class can see.

If the classroom is not equipped with computers, the teacher may have students bring their own portable computers to class so that they can work individually or in small groups of 2 to 3 on the CD-ROM activities during designated class hours. CD-ROM activities may also be assigned as homework.

Suggestions for Teachers

We recommend that teachers

- spend 4-5 hours on each lesson in the Textbook and 2 hours on each lesson in the CD-ROM. The course materials and lesson length may be adjusted according to students' proficiency level and learning ability.
- allocate 1-2 class hours to go over with students the Review units in the Workbook as a way to check on the students' progress.
- have students complete 1-2 pages of the Workbook after every two class sessions.
- encourage students to spend 10 minutes a day on the Sentence Quiz in the CD-ROM. Practice makes perfect!

More Support

IQChinese is the publisher for *IQChinese Go* multimedia CD-ROMs. By adopting Type-To-Learn as its core methodology, IQChinese provides learners of the Chinese language a complete solution to learn the language effectively.

Courseware & Homework

IQChinese offers additional resources for both teachers and students:

eClass (http://eclass.iqchinese.com): offers additional lesson-by-lesson practices, and allows teachers to create own assignments and quizzes.

IQChinese Fun (http://www.iqchinesefun.com): visit the website or use mobile applications for iPhone, iPad, and iPod Touch to learn and practice Chinese characters in a fun and interesting way.

- "Type-to-Learn" courseware for PC & Mac
- textbook & workbook
- online practice system
- mobile practice apps for iOS
- Chinese learning software

Teaching Support

Online teacher workshops, additional classroom activities and resources such as detailed chapter-by-chapter lesson plans, teaching slides, and supplementary assignments are developed to facilitate classroom teaching. Visit the following websites for more information.

Cengage Learning http://www.cengageasia.com

IQChinese Teacher's Club http://www.iqchinese.com

- online teaching resources
- teacher training & workshops
- supporting software

Technical Support

IQChinese offers technical support for product installation, school site licensing, digital lesson planning, etc. If you require technical assistance, please contact iqservice@iqchinese.com

- product installation
- school site license
- digital learning conversion
- digital teaching planning

Scope & Sequence

Lesson	Communicative Goals	Vocabulary	Language Usage	Cultural Information
我的家人 My Family **1**	• Be familiar with the terms of address of my family members and relatives • Introduce my family members and relatives and describe our relationships	**Terms of address of family members and relatives** 爺爺, 奶奶, 伯伯, 叔叔, 姑姑, 堂哥, 堂妹, 表姊, 表弟, 外公, 外婆, 舅舅, 姨媽, 表哥, 表妹, 孫子, 外孫, 一家人, 外孫女, 女兒, 兒子, 男, 孫女, 同…	• **Usage of "都是" and "就是"** 哥哥、弟弟和我都是爸媽的兒子。 爸爸的爸爸就是我的爺爺。 • **Sentence pattern "是……,也是……"** 他是我的中文老師,也是哥哥的中文老師。 • **Usage of "同 / 一樣"** 我們看同一本書。 我們看一樣的書。 • **Chinese radicals "女" and "言"**	• Differences in paternal and maternal terms of address stemmed from favoritism of males in ancient, agriculture-based China. • Chinese terms of address are an expression of respect for the elders.
學校活動 School Activities **2**	• State my extra-curricular activities • Express which extra-curricular activities I would like to participate in • Use conjunction "可是" to convey a particular tone or to indicate a contrast in meaning	**Participating in school activities** 學校, 上課, 下課, 樂隊, 球隊, 課外活動, 參加, 回家, 想, 休息, 可是, 得 (děi), 送, 給…	• **Usage of "要 / 想"** 我要去上學。 我想去上學。 • **Usage of "得 (děi)"** 我在學校得上課,還得參加課外活動。 • **Usage of conjunction "可是"** 我想休息,可是功課還沒做。 • **Sentence patterns "送…… / 送了……給……"** 爺爺送奶奶一台電腦。 爺爺送了一台電腦給奶奶。 • **Usage of Chinese punctuation ":" and "「」"** 表妹說:「昨天奶奶送了一個背包給我。」	
用心做好 Try Your Best **3**	• Explain the importance of trying one's best in what he does • State if one is able or unable to complete a certain task • Use adjectives in the superlative	**Grades and examinations** 作業, 壞, 交, 大考, 小考, 完, 成績, 重要, 用心, 最, 考, 時候, 得 (de)…	• **Sentence patterns "Verb + 不完 / Verb + 完了"** 桌上的飯菜很多,我吃不完。 桌上的飯菜我都吃完了。 • **Usage of adverbial "最"** 小明寫的字最好看。 • **Turning adjectives into questions** 重要 → 重不重要? • **Sentence pattern "什麼時候……?"** 我什麼時候來接你? • **Chinese radical "心"**	

Lesson	Communicative Goals	Vocabulary	Language Usage	Cultural Information
我生病了 I Am Sick 4	• Describe my symptoms to the doctor • Inquire after someone else, or inquire about the cause of a condition • Describe actions	**Sickness and recovery** 流鼻水, 咳嗽, 醫生, 藥, 水, 鼻水, 流, 咳, 難過, 生病, 怎麼, 出來, 出去…	• **Usage of "得"** 表妹咳嗽咳得真難過。 • **Sentence pattern "不……，不會……"** 不吃藥，病不會好。 • **Sentence patterns "怎麼了？/ 怎麼……？"** 你怎麼了？ 你怎麼沒寫作業？ • **Usage of "出來 / 出去"** 弟弟生病，鼻水從鼻子流出來了。 媽媽每天早上都出去買菜。	• How traditional Chinese physicians examine their patients • Evolution of Chinese characters—pictographic characters and associative compounds
家在哪裡？ Where Is Your Home? 5	• Ask for directions to a particular destination • Give directions to a particular location • Describe the location of a place	**Description of the locations of common facilities** 飯館, 市場, 停車場, 醫院, 圖書館, 球場, 向, 左轉, 向前, 附近, 方便, 對面, 住, 停車, 買菜, 離, 近, 看病, 右轉…	• **Usage of "有 / 在"** 我家後面有圖書館。 圖書館在我家後面。 • **Sentence pattern "……在哪裡？"** 請問市場在哪裡？ • **Sentence pattern "從……到……" (location)** 從我家到市場要走十五分鐘。 • **Sentence pattern "去 (somewhere)(do something)"** 我去圖書館看書。 • **Linking prepositions of location and their usage** 九百個上下。 八百五十個左右。	• The traditional folklore, *The Three Moves of Mencius' Mother* • The common use of "東" (east), "西" (west), "南" (south), and "北" (north) in giving directions in some Chinese cities
我的心情 My Moods 6	• Express my emotions and moods • Explain the cause of or reason for something	**Description of emotions and moods** 開心, 心情, 難過, 生氣, 吵架, 打架, 美麗, 難看, 罵人, 自己, 帶, 因為, 所以, 為什麼…	• **Usage of "自己"** 我自己會做飯、洗衣服。 • **Sentence pattern "因為……，所以……"** 因為我生病了，所以我沒去上學。 • **Usage of "為什麼"** 你為什麼心情不好？ 為什麼你心情不好？ 你心情不好，為什麼？ • **Positions of Chinese radicals**	• Concealment of ill feelings is a cultural expectation of Chinese to maintain social harmony.
我看球賽 Watching a Ball Game 7	• Express my feelings when watching a ball game • Describe the results of a ball game • Make comparisons between two subjects	**Description of the happenings and feelings during a ball game** 棒球, 籃球, 桌球/兵乓球, 比賽, ……隊, 贏, 輸, 精彩, 球賽, 緊張, 比, 分, 喜歡, 場, 運動, 票…	• **Usage of "比"** 十比七，紅隊贏，藍隊輸。 我比表弟大兩歲。 • **Usage of "比一比"** 我們來比一比，看誰打得好。 • **Chinese character "青"**	• A display of chivalry and sportsmanship by noblemen was often seen in Archery competitions in ancient China.

Lesson	Communicative Goals	Vocabulary	Language Usage	Cultural Information
我的愛好 My Hobbies **8**	• Talk about my hobbies • Ask about others' hobbies • Use time adverbials to indicate frequency • Describe two simultaneous actions in the same sentence	**Description of hobbies** 唱歌, 跳舞, 音樂, 跑步, 愛好, 常常, 朋友, 次, 一邊……, 一邊……, 每次, 小時…	• **Usage of time adverbial "常常"** 表妹喜歡跳舞，她常常參加跳舞比賽。 • **Sentence pattern "一邊……，一邊……"** 姊姊一邊走路，一邊唱歌。 • **Expansion of phrases** 上課 → 上什麼課？ • **Characters with more than one form of pronunciation** 好： 很好 (hǎo) 　　 愛好 (hào)	
電視節目 Television Programs **9**	• Talk about my favorite television programs • Ask about others' favorite television programs • Express one's compliance with another person's decision or action • Express the sequence of occurrence between two actions or events	**Categories of television programs** 電視(機), 節目表, 新聞, 卡通, 電影, 打開, 節目, 加, 英文, 選, 久, 種…	• **Usage of "很久 / 太久"** 我找了很久，還是找不到圖書館。 弟弟電視看得太久了，所以作業還沒寫完。 • **Usage of "就" (where the second clause replicates the first clause)** 你看哪個節目，我就看哪個節目。 • **Usage of "再"** 看完電影，再去圖書館。 • **Homophones** shì：是, 事, 市, 視	• The similar pronunciation of "書" (book) and "輸" (to lose) makes books an unlucky gift for some Chinese because they believe the gift will cause a loss of something.
今天天氣 The Weather Today **10**	• Describe the weather • Describe feelings of hot and cold • Describe an ongoing action or two actions that are occurring concurrently	**Description of the weather** 太陽, 陽光, 颱風, 下雨, 晴天, 陰天, 熱, 冷, 著, 笑, 張著, 樹, 外面…	• **Usage of "著"** 姑姑聽著音樂跳舞。 • **Sentence pattern "……怎麼樣？"** 今天天氣怎麼樣？ • **Usage of "會 + adjective"** 明天會很熱嗎？ 我想明天會很熱。 • **Hypothetical sentences with "如果 / 要是" (if) omitted** 明天天氣好，我們就去打球。 • **Usage of chinese punctuation "；"** 明天出太陽，我們就去球場打球；下雨，我們就在家裡玩遊戲。	

xii　Scope & Sequence

Table of Contents

我的家人
My Family

My Goals

1 Be familiar with the terms of address of my family members and relatives
2 Understand the differences between the paternal and maternal family in the Chinese society
3 Be able to introduce my family members and relatives and describe our relationships
4 Understand how radicals can classify Chinese characters into various semantic categories

Get Started

yé ye 爺爺   nǎi nai 奶奶

bó bo 伯伯   bó mǔ 伯母*   爸爸   gū zhàng 姑丈*   gū gu 姑姑   shú shu 叔叔   shěn shen 嬸嬸*

táng gē 堂哥   táng mèi 堂妹

biǎo mèi 表妹

你好！我是謝小明，
他們是我的家人。

我   妹妹

*伯母 aunt (wife of father's older brother)   *姑丈 uncle (husband of father's sister)   *嬸嬸 aunt (wife of father's younger brother)

New Words

yé ye 爺爺 grandfather (paternal)   nǎi nai 奶奶 grandmother (paternal)   bó bo 伯伯 uncle (father's older brother)   shú shu 叔叔 uncle (father's younger brother)

gū gu 姑姑 aunt (father's sister)   táng gē 堂哥 older cousin (male, paternal)   táng mèi 堂妹 younger cousin (female, maternal)   biǎo mèi 表妹 younger cousin (female, both paternal & maternal)

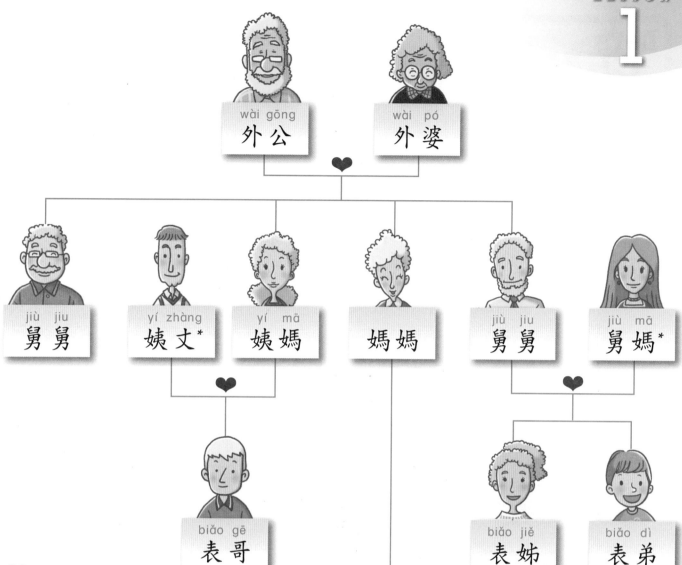

弟弟

**Work It Out**

1 Apart from "爸爸", "媽媽", "哥哥", "姊姊", "弟弟", and "妹妹", which other relatives do you have?

2 On your computer, create your family tree and insert the Chinese terms of address of all your relatives. E-mail your teacher or print out the family tree.

*姨丈 uncle (husband of mother's sister)　　*舅媽 aunt (wife of mother's brother)

New Words

wài gōng 外公 grandfather (maternal)	wài pó 外婆 grandmother (maternal)	jiù jiu 舅舅 uncle (mother's brother)	yí mā 姨媽 aunt (mother's sister)
biǎo gē 表哥 older cousin (male, both paternal & maternal)	biǎo jiě 表姊 older cousin (female, both paternal & maternal)	biǎo dì 表弟 younger cousin (male, both paternal & maternal)	

yé ye nǎi nai   sūn zi
爺爺奶奶愛孫子，

wài gōng wài pó   wài sūn
外公外婆愛外孫，

sūn zi wài sūn
孫子外孫都是我，

yì jiā rén
大家都是一家人。

New Words

sūn zi
孫子 grandson (son's son)

wài sūn
外孫 grandson (daughter's son)

yì jiā rén
一家人 the whole family

TIP

"外" connotes something "external" and "distant". In traditional Chinese societies, when a girl gets married, she is no longer considered part of her family as she will take on her husband's surname. Her children are then known as "外孫" and "外孫女" to her parents, and her children address their maternal grandparents as "外公" and "外婆". Today, Chinese women do not necessarily take on their husband's surname upon marriage, but the maternal terms of address remain unchanged.

Why are your father's brothers differentiated by the terms "伯伯" and "叔叔" while your mother's brothers are known simply as "舅舅"?

Historically, China depended largely on agriculture, which required a lot of labor. Hence, Chinese families favored males as they could provide the manual labor on the farms. This has led to the patriarchal Chinese society we see today where the paternal terms of address are more elaborate and detailed.

Let's Learn GRAMMAR

都是

哥哥、弟弟和我都是爸媽的<ruby>兒子<rt>ér zi</rt></ruby>。

我家除了媽媽，都是<ruby>男<rt>nán</rt></ruby>的。

媽媽和<ruby>姨媽<rt>yí mā</rt></ruby>都是<ruby>外公<rt>wài gōng</rt></ruby>的<ruby>女兒<rt>nǚ ér</rt></ruby>。

New Words

<ruby>兒子<rt>ér zi</rt></ruby> son

<ruby>男<rt>nán</rt></ruby> male

<ruby>女兒<rt>nǚ ér</rt></ruby> daughter

<ruby>孫女<rt>sūn nǚ</rt></ruby> granddaughter (son's daughter)

<ruby>外孫女<rt>wài sūn nǚ</rt></ruby> granddaugther (daughter's daughter)

就是

爸爸的爸爸就是我的<ruby>爺爺<rt>yé ye</rt></ruby>。

媽媽的媽媽就是我的<ruby>外婆<rt>wài pó</rt></ruby>。

是⋯⋯，也是⋯⋯

他是我的中文老師，也是哥哥的中文老師。

我是爸爸的<ruby>女兒<rt>nǚ ér</rt></ruby>，也是<ruby>奶奶<rt>nǎi nai</rt></ruby>的<ruby>孫女<rt>sūn nǚ</rt></ruby>。

我是媽媽的<ruby>女兒<rt>nǚ ér</rt></ruby>，也是<ruby>外公<rt>wài gōng</rt></ruby>的<ruby>外孫女<rt>wài sūn nǚ</rt></ruby>。

tóng
同 / 一樣

New Words

tóng
同 the same

táng gē tóng
我和堂哥同姓，我們都姓謝。

nǎi nai   táng mèi   nǎi nai   tóng
我的奶奶和堂妹的奶奶是同一個人。

tóng
我們看同一本書。

我們看一樣的書。

Think and Answer

Check the box next to the sentence that accurately describes the quantity of bread as depicted in each picture.

tóng
① 小明和大關吃同一個麵包。

他們吃 ➔ □ 一個麵包
       ➔ □ 兩個麵包

② 小明和大關吃一樣的麵包。

他們吃 ➔ □ 一個麵包
       ➔ □ 兩個麵包

Go300

WANT TO LEARN MORE?

Check out the Text > Sentence Pattern section in the Go300 CD.

Find a partner and practice the following dialogues.

⭐Task 1

Ⓐ：昨天你和誰一起打球？

Ⓑ：我表弟。
biǎo dì

Ⓐ：他是你叔叔的兒子嗎？
shú shu　ér zi

Ⓑ：不是。他是我舅舅的兒子，也是我的同學。
jiù jiu　ér zi

⭐Task 2

Ⓐ：我堂哥大我兩歲，堂妹小我一歲。
táng gē　táng mèi

你有堂哥、堂妹嗎？
táng gē　táng mèi

Ⓑ：我有堂哥，沒有堂妹。
táng gē　táng mèi

我堂哥也大我兩歲。
táng gē

Ⓐ：我們的堂哥一樣大，
táng gē

都是十五歲。

TIP
"大我兩歲"
means someone is two
years older than I;
"小我一歲" means
someone is one year
younger than I.

TIP The Chinese are very respectful towards their elders and do not address them by their names. Instead they address them by the proper terms of address, even including the rank of their elders in terms of the seniority among his or her siblings (二伯, 三姑).

Because China covers a vast land, terms of address may vary slightly across different regions. For example, one's father's sisters may be known as "姑姑" in one region and "姑媽" in another. One's mother's sisters may be called "姨媽", "姨", or "阿姨" according to the norm in different regions.

Task 3

Ⓐ : _____

Ⓑ : 我有三個姑姑，
我叫她們大姑姑、
二姑姑和小姑姑。

Task 4

Ⓐ : 爸爸的爸爸就是我的爺爺。
我和爺爺同姓，我們都姓謝。

Ⓑ : 你堂哥也姓謝嗎？

Ⓐ : 對，我們同姓。堂哥和我都是爺爺的孫子。

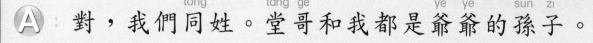

The following dialogues are adapted from the Text > Dialogue section in your Go300. Listen to the CD before reading the transcript on this page.

⭐ Task 5

Ⓐ 你的堂弟、堂妹多大了？
táng dì táng mèi

Ⓑ 我的堂弟今年十二歲，堂妹今年十歲。
táng dì táng mèi

⭐ Task 6

Ⓐ 你的爺爺、奶奶有幾個孫子、孫女？
yé ye nǎi nai sūn zi sūn nǚ

Ⓑ 我的爺爺、奶奶有四個孫子、兩個孫女。
yé ye nǎi nai sūn zi sūn nǚ

⭐ Task 7

Ⓐ 你和誰一起去外公、
外婆家？
wài gōng
wài pó

Ⓑ 我和表哥、表姊一起去。
biǎo gē biǎo jiě

Ⓐ 你的外公、外婆都在家嗎？
wài gōng wài pó

Ⓑ 是，他們都在家。

⭐ Extend Dialogues

Work in pairs and take turns to extend the dialogues in tasks 5 to 7. If you were A, which of the questions below would you select to continue each dialogue? If you were B, how would you answer the final question in each dialogue?

(1) 你爺爺的孫女和你同姓嗎？

(2) 你在外公、外婆家玩什麼遊戲？

(3) 你的堂弟比堂妹大幾歲？

A big difference between English words and Chinese characters is that while English words are made up of letters of the alphabet, Chinese characters are composed of radicals and individual components. Each radical carries a certain attribute or meaning. So we can deduce the meaning of a character by looking at its semantic association indicated by its radicals. This lesson introduces the radicals "女" and "言".

nǚ

女

The radical "女" is typically related to femininity. The character "女" looks just like a female kneeling on the ground with both hands crossed in front of her.

pó

婆

gū

姑

yí

姨

媽

yán

言

The radical "言" is commonly associated with speech. In ancient times before the writing system was established, people used to draw a mouth with curved lines radiating from it to signify sound waves. This has evolved to the earliest form of the character "言".

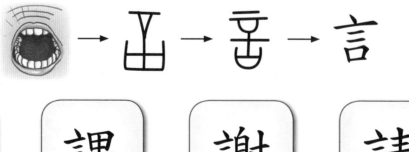

說

課

謝

請

Text 1 Go 300

Read the following text carefully.

yé ye 爺爺今年八十六歲，nǎi nai 奶奶今年八十二歲，

sūn zi 他們有七個孫子、sūn nǔ 兩個孫女、

wài sūn 三個外孫和wài sūn nǔ 一個外孫女。

yé ye nǎi nai 爺爺奶奶說他們很幸福，

他們能吃、能喝、能聽、能看、能走，

可以天天和我們zài yì qǐ在一起*，這就是幸福。

*在一起 stay together

Answer these questions in Chinese.

1 By how many years is Grandfather older than Grandmother?

2 How many children do the grandparents have in total?

3 Why do the grandparents feel very fortunate?

4 Does the author have a "姑姑"? How can you tell?

Read the following text carefully.

我爺爺胖胖的、矮矮的。
（yé ye）

他愛吃麵，不愛吃麵包。

> "會" here indicates the capability of a person who has gone through some training or practice.

爺爺很能幹，他會說中文，有時他教我說中文；
（yé ye）

他會開車，有時他送我去上學。

爺爺有一個兒子、一個女兒、兩個孫女和三個
（yé ye）（ér zi）（nǚ ér）（sūn nǚ）

外孫。我們常常*一起吃飯，一起出去玩。
（wài sūn）（cháng cháng）

爺爺今年八十歲了，他會用電腦寫電子郵件*，
（yé ye）（diàn zǐ yóu jiàn）

還會玩電腦遊戲。我愛我的爺爺，我的爺爺也愛我。
（yé ye）（yé ye）

*常常 often
*電子郵件 e-mail

Answer these questions in Chinese.

1   How many sons, daughters, grandsons, and granddaughters does the author's grandfather have respectively?

2   If the author is 15 years old, how much younger is he than his grandfather?

3   According to the description in the text, which of the following statements is <u>incorrect</u>?

☐   The author dosen't have an uncle.

☐   The author has an aunt.

☐   The author is a female.

WANT TO LEARN MORE?

Check out the Text > Reading section in the Go300 CD.

Study the family tree below and answer the questions on the following page.

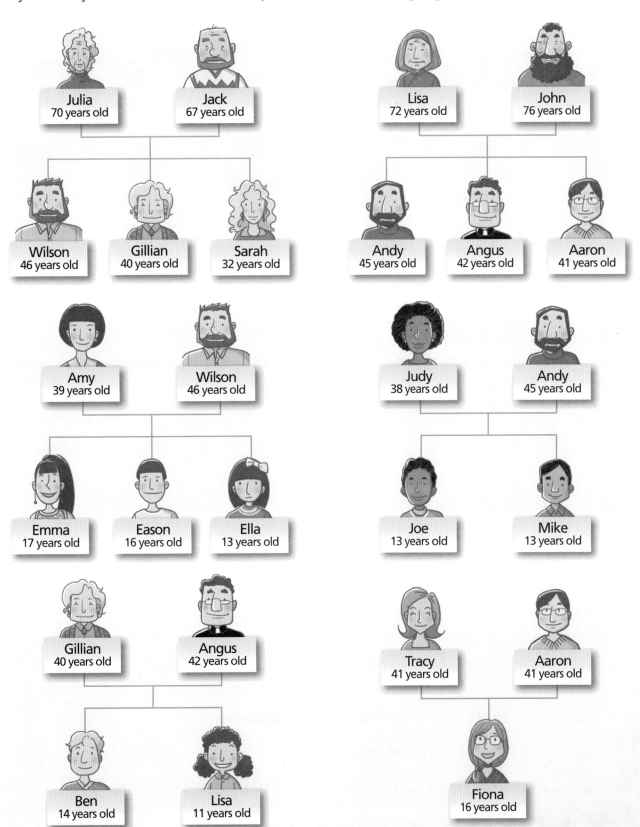

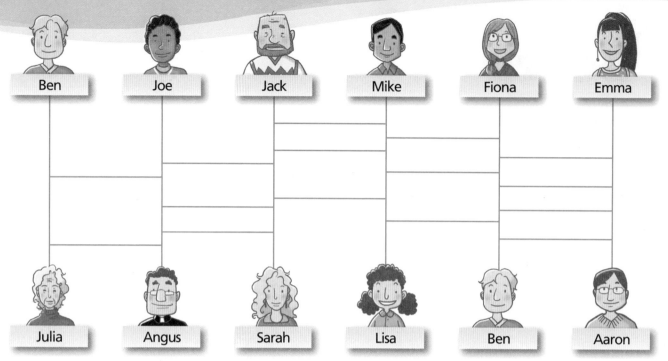

1 According to the diagram above, start with a character in the bottom row and trace the line from this character upwards, turning at <u>every</u> fork you encounter. You will be able to link the character to another character in the top row. For example, Julia will be connected to Ben.

2 State the relationship between the two characters by looking at the family tree on the previous page.

For example, "Julia 是 Ben 的外婆。"
wài pó

3 From the six pairs of characters formed, select three pairs and record their relationships in Chinese in the blanks below.

①	
②	
③	

LEARNING LOG

I can...	Excellent	Good	Fair	Needs Improvement
1 address my family members and relatives by their correct titles in Chinese.	☐	☐	☐	☐
2 differentiate the terms of address between my paternal and maternal families.	☐	☐	☐	☐
3 use "就是", "都是", and "也是" appropriately in sentences.	☐	☐	☐	☐
4 recognize that characters with the radical "女" are commonly related to femininity; characters with the radical "言" are commonly associated with speech.	☐	☐	☐	☐
5 write "外", "公", "婆", "女", and "孫".	☐	☐	☐	☐

2

學校活動
School Activities

My Goals

1   Become familiar with the names of extra-curricular activities in school
2   Be able to express which extra-curricular activity I can or would like to participate in
3   Be able to use conjunction "可是" to convey a particular tone or to indicate a contrast in meaning
4   Become familiar with Chinese punctuation "：" and "「　」"
5   Become familiar with vocabulary associated with participating in school activities

xué xiào
學校

shàng kè
上課

xià kè
下課

yuè duì
樂隊

qiú duì
球隊

lā lā duì
啦啦隊
(cheerleading)

qí yì shè
棋藝社
(chess club)

hé chàng tuán
合唱團
(choir)

xué shēng huì
學生會
(student union)

⭐ Work It Out

1 What extra-curricular activities have you participated in this year? What made you take part in these activities? What other extra-curricular activities would you like to engage in?

2 Imagine you are a reporter. Using after-class hours, interview three of your classmates. Ask them what their extra-curricular activities are and why they choose to participate in them. Record your interviews using any recording device.

New Words

xué xiào	shàng kè	xià kè	yuè duì	qiú duì
學校 school	上課 go to class	下課 end of class	樂隊 music band	球隊 ball team

xué xiào kè wài huó dòng
學校課外活動多，

cān jiā yuè duì
參加樂隊還打球，

xià kè huí jiā xiǎng xiū xí
下課回家想休息，

kě shì děi
可是還得做功課。

New Words

kè wài huó dòng 課外活動 extra-curricular activity	cān jiā 參加 join; participate in	huí jiā 回家 go home	xiǎng 想 want

xiū xí 休息 rest	kě shì 可是 but, however	děi 得 have to

Let's Learn GRAMMAR

TIP "要" indicates the intention to actually do something. "想" indicates a consideration or a wish to do something. In a sentence, what follows "要" or "想" is the action that has not yet been fulfilled. Semantically, "要" is more forceful than "想" as the actual fulfillment of the action that occurs after "要" is more certain.

要 / 想(xiǎng)

我要去上學。

我要參加課外活動。(cān jiā kè wài huó dòng)

我要休息。(xiū xí)

我想(xiǎng)去上學。

我想參加課外活動。(xiǎng cān jiā kè wài huó dòng)

我想休息。(xiǎng xiū xí)

得(děi)

我得(děi)做好功課再去玩。

爸爸得(děi)上班賺錢。

弟弟得(děi)去上學。

TIP When "得" is pronounced děi, what follows the word (得) has to be an action that should or must be done.

我在學校得上課(xué xiào děi shàng kè)，還得參加課外活動(děi cān jiā kè wài huó dòng)。

今天我得(děi)掃落葉，還得(děi)教弟弟做功課。

kě shì
可是

xiǎng xiū xí　　kě shì
我想休息，可是功課還沒做。

xiǎng　　　　　kě shì
他想吃三明治，可是沒有錢。

xiǎng　　　　　　kě shì
小明想買這本書，可是書太貴了。

| 爺爺 | sòng 送 | 奶奶 | 一台電腦。 |

sòng
姑姑送表弟一雙鞋。

sòng
叔叔送堂哥一張桌子。

| 爺爺 | sòng 送了 | 一台電腦 | gěi 給 | 奶奶。 |

sòng　　　　gěi
表哥送了一枝筆給表妹。

sòng　　　　gěi
外公送了一本書給外婆。

Want More Practice?

Fit the sentences on the left into the other sentence structure ("送了……給……" or "送") and practice reading them.

New Words

sòng
送 give (as a present)

gěi
給 give

Go300

WANT TO LEARN MORE?

Check out the Text > Sentence Pattern section in the Go300 CD.

Find a partner and practice the following dialogues.

★ Task 1

外公的生日 (birthday) 到了，你想送外公什麼？

我想送他一張卡片 (card)。你想送什麼？

我也想送一張卡片給他。

你想在卡片上寫什麼？

_____。

★ Task 2

你參加什麼學校活動？

我參加了樂隊，你參加什麼？

我參加了球隊。

除了樂隊，我也想參加球隊。

⭐ Task 3

Ⓐ：明天早上你來我家玩，好不好？

Ⓑ：我很想去，可是明天早上我得上中文課。
xiǎng kě shì děi

Ⓐ：明天下午我們一起去打球，好不好？

Ⓑ：我很想去，可是我參加了球隊，下午我得在
xiǎng kě shì cān jiā qiú duì děi
學校打球。
xué xiào

Ⓐ：我也想參加球隊。參加了球隊，我們就可以
xiǎng cān jiā qiú duì cān jiā qiú duì
一起打球了。

⭐ Task 4

Ⓐ：你們學校有什麼課外活動？
xué xiào kè wài huó dòng

Ⓑ：＿＿＿＿＿＿＿＿＿＿＿＿＿＿＿。

Ⓐ：你參加什麼課外活動？
cān jiā kè wài huó dòng

Ⓑ：＿＿＿＿＿＿＿＿＿＿＿＿＿＿＿。

The following dialogues are adapted from the Text > Dialogue section in your  Go300 . Listen to the CD before reading the transcript on this page.

⭐ Task 5

Ⓐ : 這個星期天你有什麼活動？
_{huó dòng}

Ⓑ : 星期天下午，我要和同學一起去打球。

⭐ Task 6

Ⓐ : 你參加什麼課外活動？
_{cān jiā}   _{kè wài huó dòng}

Ⓑ : 我參加了樂隊，還有球隊。
_{cān jiā}   _{yuè duì}   _{qiú duì}

⭐ Task 7

Ⓐ : 我們要去打球，你想不想一起去？
_{xiǎng}   _{xiǎng}

Ⓑ : 我想去，可是功課太多，不能去。
_{xiǎng}   _{kě shì}

⭐ Task 8

Ⓐ : 你舅舅星期六上班嗎？

Ⓑ : 不上班，他星期六在家休息。
_{xiū xí}

Let's Learn PUNCTUATION

：
mào hào
冒 號
(colon)

When a colon is placed after a name or a term of address, what follows is usually the speech of that person. When it is placed after a collective phrase, what follows is commonly an elaboration or explanation of that collective phrase.

The colon can also be used together with quotation marks (「 」). Placed after words such as "說" or "問", they contain the content of one's speech or question.

小明：你媽媽在家嗎？

大關：不在，她去上班了。

　　　　　　　cān jiā　　　　　xué xiào huó dòng　　qiú duì　　yuè duì
我參加了兩個學校活動：球隊和樂隊。

　　　　　　　　　　sòng　　　　　　　　gěi
表妹說：「昨天奶奶送了一個背包給我。」

「 」
yǐn hào
引 號
(quotation marks)

Quotation marks can be used together with the colon to draw out the content of what a person is saying or asking. If there is an emphasis in a sentence, quotation marks can also be used to focus the reader's attention on the key point.

　　　　　　　　　　　　　　　　　　nǚ
「媽」和「姑」這兩個字都有「女」，媽媽和姑姑都

　nǚ
是女 (female) 的。

Practice It

Fill in the blanks with the correct punctuation marks.

　　　　　　xiǎng xiū xí
① 小明問□□你想休息嗎□□

② □說□和□課□這兩個字都有□言□□

 **Text 1** 💿 Go 300

Read the following text carefully.

kè wài huó dòng
課外活動我都愛，

yuè duì
星期一、星期三和星期五，有樂隊，

星期二和星期四，要打球，

xià kè huí jiā xiǎng xiū xí
下課回家想休息，

媽媽叫我做功課，

奶奶叫我寫中文，

從早到晚忙忙忙，真辛苦。

Answer these questions in Chinese.

1　On which days does the author <u>not</u> have ball practice?
　　On which days does the author <u>not</u> have band practice?

2　What does the author wish to do when he gets home?

3　Who wants the author to practice writing Chinese
　　when he gets home?

Read the following text carefully.

　　　　　　xué xiào　　　　　　　shàng kè　　　　　　　　　huó dòng　　yuè
在學校，除了要上課，還有很多活動。有樂
duì　　qiú duì　　lā lā duì　　　　xué shēng huì
隊、球隊、啦啦隊，還有學生會。

　　　　　　　　　　　　　　　　　shàng kè　　kě shì
星期六、星期日不用上課，可是我和小明都
　　　　cān jiā　　　　　　kè wài huó dòng　yuè duì　　qiú duì
很忙。我們參加一樣的課外活動：樂隊和球隊。

　　　　　　　　shàng kè　　　　　　cān jiā huó dòng　měi yí ge
我和小明一起上課，一起參加活動。每一個*
huó dòng　　　　　měi yí ge huó dòng
活動都好玩，每一個活動我們都愛。

*每一個 each one of

Answer these questions in Chinese.

1　What extra-curricular activities does the author participate in?

2　On which days do the author and 小明 engage in their extra-curricular activities?

3　Does the author enjoy being in the music band and on the ball team? How can you tell?

4　Does the author think that a student's life is hectic? As a student, are you busy? Why?

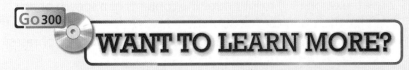

Go300

WANT TO LEARN MORE?

Check out the Text > Reading section in the Go300 CD.

The societies in school are recruiting members.

Mary, Julie, and Lily wish to join the same society. The following table shows you the schedule of their present extra-curricular activities. Study it, and with the help of the posters provided, complete the conversation below.

	星期日	星期一	星期二	星期三	星期四	星期五	星期六
Mary			中文課		電腦課		
Julie				學生會 xué shēng huì		合唱團 hé chàng tuán	
Lilly	中文課					合唱團 hé chàng tuán	

Julie ：我要參加啦啦隊，你們想和我一起參加嗎？
cān jiā lā lā duì cān jiā

Mary ：_____ （可是）
kě shì

Lilly ：_____ （可是）
kě shì

_____ （一起）

LEARNING LOG	I can...	Excellent	Good	Fair	Needs Improvement
	1 state the names of common extra-curricular activities.	☐	☐	☐	☐
	2 use "想" to express my desires.	☐	☐	☐	☐
	3 use "可是" to convey a particular tone or to indicate a contrast in meaning.	☐	☐	☐	☐
	4 list the reasons for participating in certain extra-curricular activities.	☐	☐	☐	☐
	5 use the colon (：) to introduce the contents of a speech or an explanation, and use the quotation marks (「 」) to contain the contents of a speech or to emphasize certain words and phrases.	☐	☐	☐	☐
	6 write "校", "活", "動", "想", and "給".	☐	☐	☐	☐

3

用心做好
Try Your Best

My Goals

1 Be able to explain the importance of trying one's best in what he does

2 Be able to express if one is able or unable to complete a certain task

3 Be able to use adjectives in the superlative

4 Become familiar with the radical "心" (heart)

5 Become familiar with vocabulary associated with classes, examinations, and grades

kǎo shì
考試
(examination)

kǎo juàn
考卷
(test paper)

chéng jī dān
成績單
(school report card)

zuò yè
寫作業
(do homework)

bào gào
報告
(report)

New Words

zuò yè
作業 homework

huài
壞 bad

好

huài
壞/不好

上課還要交作業，
jiāo zuò yè

大考小考忙不完，
dà kǎo xiǎo kǎo　　　wán

成績好壞不重要，
chéng jī　huài　zhòng yào

用心做好最重要。
yòng xīn　　zuì zhòng yào

★ Think About It

Do you think grades matter? Do your parents share your view?

Are grades crucial to gaining entry into a school? What other criteria will schools consider in entry applications? Why do you think these criteria matter?

Think about it and ask around — what do your classmates think about grades?

New Words

jiāo	dà kǎo	xiǎo kǎo	wán
交 hand in	大考 final examination	小考 quiz	完 finished

chéng jī	zhòng yào	yòng xīn	zuì
成績 grades	重要 important	用心 pay attention	最 most

Let's Learn GRAMMAR

Verb + 不完_{wán}/Verb + 完_{wán}了

學校大考_{dà kǎo}、小考_{xiǎo kǎo}多，我忙不完_{wán}。

桌上飯菜很多，我吃不完_{wán}。

星期五我就考完_{kǎo wán}了。

桌上的飯菜我都吃完_{wán}了。

最_{zuì}

最小_{zuì}　　　　　最大_{zuì}

小明寫的字最_{zuì}好看。

我有五個杯子，這個杯子最大_{zuì}。

哥哥、弟弟和我，弟弟的成績_{chéng jì}最_{zuì}好。

TIP
When comparing three or more subjects, you should use "最 + adjective" to express the adjective in the superlative (the highest or lowest degree).

Let's Learn GRAMMAR

Verb + 不完 (wán) / Verb + 完了 (wán)

學校大考 (dà kǎo)、小考 (xiǎo kǎo) 多，我忙不完 (wán)。

桌上飯菜很多，我吃不完 (wán)。

星期五我就考完了 (kǎo wán)。

桌上的飯菜我都吃完了 (wán)。

最 (zuì)

最小 (zuì)　　　　　最大 (zuì)

小明寫的字最 (zuì) 好看。

我有五個杯子，這個杯子最大 (zuì)。

哥哥、弟弟和我，弟弟的成績 (chéng jì) 最 (zuì) 好。

TIP
When comparing three or more subjects, you should use "最 + adjective" to express the adjective in the superlative (the highest or lowest degree).

Turning Adjectives into Questions
AB ➡ A 不 AB ？

zhòng yào   chéng jī zhòng   zhòng yào
重要 ➡ 學校成績重不重要？

yòng xīn   yòng   yòng xīn
用心 ➡ 你上課用不用心？

好看 ➡ 這本書好不好看？

TIP

When an adjective composed of two characters (AB) is in the predicate of a sentence, it can be written in the form "A不AB" to change the sentence into a positive–negative question. To answer such a question, you just need to state if you agree with the adjective used on the subject of the question.

For example:

Question: 這本書好不好看？

Answer: 這本書很好看。 (Positive)
        這本書不好看。 (Negative)

shí hòu
什麼時候……？

shí hòu
Ⓐ：我什麼時候來接你？

Ⓑ：請你下午五點半來接我。

shí hòu
Ⓐ：你什麼時候不用上課？

Ⓑ：我星期六和星期日不用上課。

New Words

shí hòu
時候 time

WANT TO LEARN MORE?

Check out the Text > Sentence Pattern section in the Go300 CD.

Find a partner and practice the following dialogues.

⭐ Task 1

Ⓐ : 明天要交作業，你的作業寫完了嗎？
（jiāo zuò yè）（zuò yè wán）

Ⓑ : 作業又多又難(difficult)，我寫不完。
（zuò yè）（nán）（wán）

Ⓐ : 你什麼時候要寫作業？
（shí hòu）（zuò yè）

你不會的作業，我可以教你。
（zuò yè）

Ⓑ : 謝謝，下午三點半請你教我寫作業。
（zuò yè）

⭐ Task 2

Ⓐ : 你前天的考試重不重要？
（kǎo shì zhòng zhòng yào）

Ⓑ : 前天的考試是大考，很重要。
（kǎo shì dà kǎo zhòng yào）

Ⓐ : 誰考得最好？
（kǎo de zuì）

Ⓑ : 小明考得最好。小明上課很用心，
（kǎo de zuì）（yòng xīn）

老師說上課用心，就能考得好。
（yòng xīn）（kǎo de）

New Words

得 (a particle used after a verb or an adjective to express possibility or capability)
（de）

⭐Task 3

Ⓐ：哥哥，這盒_(carton)牛奶可以喝嗎？

Ⓑ：你看看上面的日期_(date)。

Ⓐ：上面寫_____，

可是今天是_____。

牛奶_____（壞了/沒壞），

_____（可以/不可以）喝。

⭐Task 4

Ⓐ：你小考考得好不好？

Ⓑ：我考得不好。

> "會" here indicates the possibility of a certain outcome.

Ⓐ：考得不好，你媽媽會生氣_(angry)嗎？

Ⓑ：媽媽說成績好壞不重要，用心做好最重要。

 **Task 5**

Complete the dialogues below according to the pictures. When you have done that, listen to the dialogues in the Text > Dialogue section in your  to compare your answers.

①

六月

	4	11	18	25
星期日			19	26
星期一	5	12 大考	20	27
星期二	6	13 大考	21	28
星期三	7	14 大考	22	29
星期四	8	15 大考	23	30
星期五	1 / 2	9	16	24
星期六	3	10	17	

shí hòu

Ⓐ：你們學校什麼時候

dà kǎo
大考？

Ⓑ：_____

②

 明天

jiāo zuò yè

Ⓐ：我交作業了，

jiāo
你交了沒有？

Ⓑ：_____

③

kǎo de

Ⓐ：你考得好不好？

Ⓑ：_____

④

chéng jī

Ⓐ：小明的成績好不好？

Ⓑ：_____

34　　用心做好

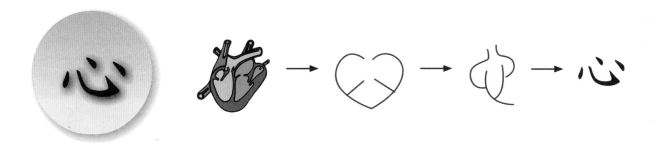

"心" is a common radical in Chinese characters. The character "心" originated from the illustration of the heart. As a radical, "心" appears in two forms: 忄 in the left-right combination and 心 in the top-bottom combination. When placed as a radical in the top-bottom combination, "心" remains unchanged in its form. However, when placed as a radical in the left-right combination, it changes from its original form into "忄", just like the case of "打" and "拿" as we have learnt earlier.

Most characters with the radical "心" are semantically related to the heart. The two characters below are both made up of a combination of the radical "心" and the component "亡", but their meanings are different. The following examples also illustrate how you can use the "Break Down Character" technique to remember these two characters.

> "亡" means "nothing" or "to perish". Imagine "忙" as the heart being so busy that it is always standing up, with no time to rest.

忙 ➡ 很忙 ➡ 我從早到晚都很忙。

> Imagine "忘" as the heart sitting down for a rest, and many things are forgotten as a result.

忘 ➡ 忘了 ➡ 我忘了今天要大考。
dà kǎo

用心做好 35

Let's READ

Text 1 Go 300

Read the following text carefully.

yòng xīn ... chéng jī
用心學，成績就會好，
kāi xīn ... kāi xīn
我開心*，爸媽也開心。
yòng xīn ... chéng jī
不用心，成績就不好，
kāi xīn ... kāi xīn
我不開心，大家都不開心。
yòng xīn ... yàng yàng ... de
用心學，小心做，樣樣*學得好，
yàng yàng ... de ... yàng yàng chéng jī
樣樣做得好，樣樣成績都會好。

* 開心 happy
* 樣樣 everything

Answer these questions in Chinese.

1 What will one achieve when he pays attention?

2 What must one do in order to do well?

3 Fill in the blanks below with "用心", "小心", and "開心".

   (a) 媽媽，＿＿＿＿＿＿！前面有車子。

   (b) 上課＿＿＿＿＿，大考＿＿＿＿＿，成績好，就很＿＿＿＿＿。

Text 2

Read the following text carefully.

老師說：「上課要用心。」

哥哥說：「做功課要用心，

參加活動要用心，玩遊戲也要用心。」

我問爸爸：「什麼是用心？」

爸爸說：「做一件*事，多聽、多問、多想，這

就是用心。」

做每一件事，做得好壞不重要，用心去做最重要。

*件 (a measure word for abstract concepts,
matters, documents, clothing, etc.)

Answer these questions in Chinese.

1   What does it mean by "用心"?

2   According to the passage, when should one pay attention?

3   Apart from what was mentioned in the text, how do you think one can pay attention?

WANT TO LEARN MORE?

Check out the Text > Reading section in the Go300 CD.

 **Reading Aloud**

The teacher will decide to use the texts from this lesson's **Let's Read** or **Let's Chant** for this activity.

1 Get into small teams. Each team has to memorize the text allocated by the teacher, and choreograph actions and group formations to accompany the recital of the text.

2 Each team will take turns to perform. The rest of the teams will grade the performing team on a total score of five with the score sheet provided below.

3 When all teams have performed their recitals, each team will comment on each of the other teams' strengths and give its score for that team. The winning team is the team with the highest total score.

	Team 1	Team 2	Team 3	Team 4
Diction				
Oral Presentation				
Choreography				
Total score				

Record of each team's strengths

I can...

		Excellent	Good	Fair	Needs Improvement
1	state what is important in preparing for an examination.	☐	☐	☐	☐
2	use "最" to express adjectives in the superlative.	☐	☐	☐	☐
3	use "Verb+完了" and "Verb+不完" appropriately in sentences.	☐	☐	☐	☐
4	explain the meaning of the radical "心", and identify the different forms of it in various characters.	☐	☐	☐	☐
5	write "考", "完", "作", "交", and "最".	☐	☐	☐	☐

4

我生病了
I Am Sick

My Goals

1 Be able to convey in simple terms the symptoms of my sickness to my doctor
2 Be able to inquire after someone else, or to inquire about the cause of a condition
3 Be able to describe actions
4 Understand how some Chinese characters evolved from illustrations
5 Become familiar with vocabulary associated with being sick

⭐ Play It

1. With your teacher, decide on accompanying actions for the vocabulary on this page.
2. Stand in three rows and number yourselves in each row according to the order of your positions.
3. The teacher will recite a series of words and phrases. The first student in each row will perform the action of the first word or phrase, the second student will perform the action for the second, and so on.
4. A wrong action or forgetting to perform an action will disqualify the student and he will have to sit down. The row with the most number of students still standing wins.

liú bí shuǐ

流鼻水

ké sòu

咳嗽

dù zi tòng

肚子痛
(stomachache)

fā shāo

發燒
(fever)

yá tòng

牙痛
(toothache)

yī shēng

醫生
(doctor)

hù shì

護士
(nurse)

bìng rén

病人
(patient)

chī yào

吃藥
(take medicine)

hē shuǐ

喝水
(drink water)

New Words

liú bí shuǐ	ké sòu	yī shēng	yào	shuǐ
流鼻水 running nose	咳嗽 cough	醫生 doctor	藥 medicine	水 water

Go 300

bí shuǐ bí shuǐ liú
鼻水鼻水流不停，

ké sòu ké　　　nán guò
咳嗽咳得真難過。

yī shēng　　　　yào
看醫生，要吃藥，

shēng bìng
生病在家多休息。

TIP

Traditional Chinese physicians examine their patients differently from the way modern doctors do with their stethoscope. Apart from asking the patients to describe their condition, traditional Chinese physicians also check and rely on the patients' appearance, breath, and pulse to determine their diagnoses. Today, these traditional methods are still practiced by many traditional Chinese physicians in the world.

The picture on page 39 shows a Chinese physician taking the pulse of a patient.

New Words

bí shuǐ
鼻水 mucus

liú
流 flow

ké
咳 cough

nán guò
難過 miserable

shēng bìng
生病 sick

Let's Learn GRAMMAR

表妹咳嗽	咳	得	真難過。

ké sòu ké dé nán guò

堂哥走路走得真快(fast)。

kuài

爸爸掃落葉掃得真辛苦。

外公學電腦學得真好。

不	吃藥，	病	不會	好。

yào

不看醫生，你的咳嗽不會好。

yī shēng　　　　ké sòu

不用心，你的成績不會好。

出來

chū lái

弟弟生病，鼻水從

shēng bìng　　bí shuǐ

鼻子(nose)流出來了。

bí zi　　liú chū lái

妹妹說：「姊姊，請你出來，

chū lái

有人找你。」

42　我生病了

^{zěn me} ^{zěn me}
怎麼了？ / 怎麼……？

^{zěn me}
你怎麼了？

^{zěn me}
小明今天沒來上學，他怎麼了？

^{zěn me} ^{shuō huà}
弟弟怎麼了，今天都沒說話 (speak)？

^{zěn me}
你怎麼沒寫作業？

^{zěn me} ^{liú bí shuǐ}
你怎麼在流鼻水？

^{zěn me}
奶奶怎麼回家？

^{zěn me}
這個問題怎麼回答？

New Words

^{zěn me}
怎麼 how

^{chū lái}
出來 come out

^{chū qù}
出去 go out

Go 300

WANT TO LEARN MORE?

Check out the Text > Sentence Pattern section in the Go300 CD.

^{chū qù}
出去

^{chū qù}
媽媽每天早上都出去
^{mǎi cài}
買菜 (buy vegetables or groceries)。

^{chū qù}
爸爸，我們出去
打球了。

我生病了　43

Find a partner and practice the following dialogues.

⭐ Task 1

Ⓐ : 你怎麼了，眼睛紅紅的？
zěn me

Ⓑ : 我的眼睛好癢(itchy)，癢得真難過。
yǎng　　yǎng de　　nán guò

Ⓐ : 你得去看醫生。
děi　　yī shēng

Ⓑ : 看了，我今天早上去看醫生了。
yī shēng

Ⓐ : 醫生說什麼？
yī shēng

Ⓑ : 醫生要我多休息。
yī shēng

> "要" here means "to ask somebody to do something".

⭐ Task 2

Ⓐ : 今天天氣很好，你怎麼不出來打球？
zěn me　　chū lái

Ⓑ : 我生病了，不能出去。
shēng bìng　　chū qù

Ⓐ : 你得去看醫生，吃了藥，
děi　　yī shēng　　yào

多休息，病就會好。
bìng

Ⓑ : 藥很難吃(tastes awful)，我不想吃藥。
yào　　nán chī　　yào

Ⓐ : 不吃藥，病不會好的。
yào　　bìng

Task 3

Doctor

Ⓐ : 你怎麼了？
　　　zěn me

Patient

Ⓑ : 我又流鼻水，又咳嗽。
　　　liú bí shuǐ　　ké sòu

Ⓐ : 你咳嗽咳了幾天了？
　　　ké sòu ké

Ⓑ : 三天了。我咳嗽咳得很難過。
　　　　　　　ké sòu ké de　nán guò

Ⓐ : 你鼻水流了幾天了？
　　　bí shuǐ liú

Ⓑ : 三天了。我鼻水也流個不停。
　　　　　　　bí shuǐ　liú

Ⓐ : 你吃一點兒藥，多休息，就會好的。
　　　　　　　yào

Ⓑ : 這個藥怎麼吃？
　　　yào zěn me

Ⓐ : 每天吃完飯，就要吃藥。
　　　　　　　　　yào

Think About It

What do you do if you catch a cold? When do you decide to see the doctor? Why?

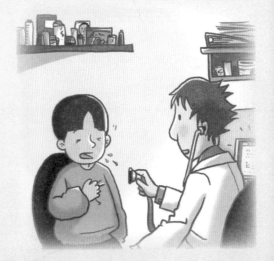

Task 4

Can you identify pairs of dialogue from the eight utterances below? Organize them into four dialogues and fill in the following table. When this is done, you may listen to the Text > Dialogue section in your Go300 for the correct answers.

①	A: 4	②	A: 2	③	A: 5	④	A: 8
	B: 1		B: 7		B: 3		B: 6

① 他考得不好，很難過。
　　　　　 nán guò

② 他看醫生了嗎？
　　 yī shēng

③ 他生病了，不能來上課。
　　 shēng bìng

④ 他怎麼了？
　　 zěn me

⑤ 他怎麼沒來上課？
　　 zěn me

⑥ 除了咳嗽，我還流鼻水，我要去看醫生。
　　　 ké sòu　　　　 liú bí shuǐ　　　　　 yī shēng

⑦ 看了，醫生要他多休息。
　　 yī shēng

⑧ 你咳嗽嗎？
　　 ké sòu

Let's Learn CHARACTER

◆ Origin of Chinese Characters

Some Chinese characters originated directly from pictorial illustrations of objects and hence are known as "象形字" (pictographic characters). Some other Chinese characters are composed of two or more components, each with a meaning of its own, to form a new character. The meaning of the new character is easily decipherable from its components and such characters are thus known as "會意字" (associative compounds). Look at the examples below. Can you tell what character each of the following illustrations has evolved into? Write it down.

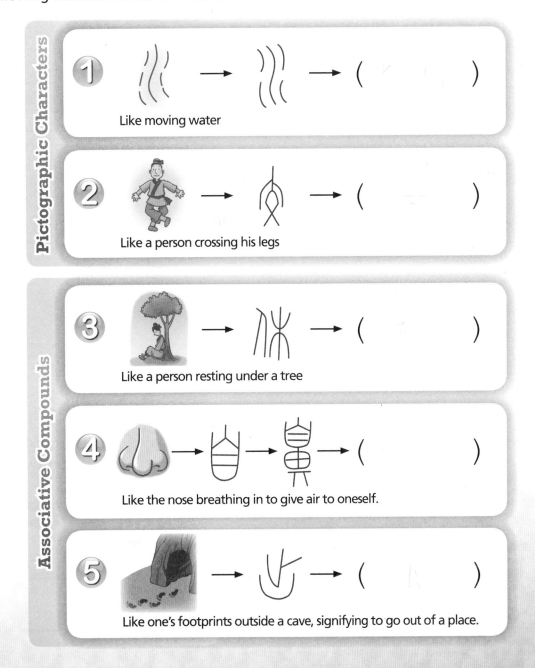

Pictographic Characters

1. Like moving water

2. Like a person crossing his legs

Associative Compounds

3. Like a person resting under a tree

4. Like the nose breathing in to give air to oneself.

5. Like one's footprints outside a cave, signifying to go out of a place.

Read the following text carefully.

我生病了，咳嗽咳個不停，鼻水也流個不停。生病很難過，我不想吃飯，也不想吃藥。可是媽媽說：不可以不吃飯，也不可以不吃藥；不吃飯，不吃藥，病就不會好。

> "吃飯" here does not merely refer to eating rice, but a full meal. Rice is the staple food for the Chinese, and so it is very apt to use "吃飯" to convey the idea of eating a full meal.

醫生說：生病要多休息。爺爺說：生病要多喝水。爸爸說：生病不要出去玩，要多休息。

Answer these questions in Chinese.

1 What symptoms does the author display?

2 What does the author's mother say he must eat when he is sick?

3 According to the author's family and doctor, what are the things that one should and should <u>not</u> do when he is sick? Write them down in the table below.

Things to do when one is sick	Things <u>not</u> to do when one is sick

Read the following text carefully.

shēng bìng
每個人都會生病，

shēng bìng　nán guò
生病很難過：

不能玩，不能上學，

不能參加活動。

shēng bìng　　　　yī shēng
生病了，要看醫生，

tīng　yī shēng de　huà
要聽醫生的話*。

bìng
病好了，就可以玩；

bìng
病好了，就可以上學；

bìng
病好了，就可以參加活動。

> Here, "就" carries an hypothetical tone. It indicates that the desired outcome can be achieved as long as the conditions stated in the preceding clause are met.

*聽醫生的話 obey the doctor's instructions

Answer these questions in Chinese.

1　Who will fall sick?
2　What do we do when we fall sick?
3　What can we do once we are well?

WANT TO LEARN MORE?

Check out the Text > Reading section in the Go300 CD.

liú bí shuǐ — 流鼻水
ké sòu — 咳嗽
fā shāo — 發燒
yá tòng — 牙痛

dù zi tòng — 肚子痛

jiǎo tòng — 腳痛 (leg pain)

1. Obtain two dice and pair up with a friend to play the roles of a doctor and a patient. The student acting as the patient will roll the dice simultaneously to determine the two symptoms of illness.

2. Match the numbers on the dice to the symptoms numbered on this page and carry out the following dialogue. If both dice yield the same number, the student acting as the doctor will say "你沒有生病，多休息就好了。".

yī shēng — 醫生： zěn me — 你怎麼了？

bìng rén — 病人：我又 liú bí shuǐ 流鼻水，又 ké sòu 咳嗽，很 nán guò 難過。

yī shēng — 醫生：你除了要吃 yào 藥，還要多喝 shuǐ 水。

吃了 yào 藥，多喝 shuǐ 水，bìng 病就會好。

LEARNING LOG	I can...	Excellent	Good	Fair	Needs Improvement
	1 state simple symptoms of sicknesses such as cough and running nose in Chinese.	☐	☐	☐	☐
	2 use "怎麼了？" to inquire after somebody else.	☐	☐	☐	☐
	3 pronounce "得" appropriately, and use "Verb + 得 + Adjective" to describe an action.	☐	☐	☐	☐
	4 identify "水" and "交" as pictographic characters.	☐	☐	☐	☐
	5 identify "休", "鼻", and "出" as associative compounds.	☐	☐	☐	☐
	6 write "水", "流", "難", "過", and "病".	☐	☐	☐	☐

家在哪裡？
Where Is Your Home?

My Goals

1 Be able to ask for directions to a particular destination
2 Be able to give directions to a particular location
3 Be able to describe the facilities surrounding a particular area
4 Become familiar with prepositions of location that look similar
5 Become familiar with the names of common facilities around my house

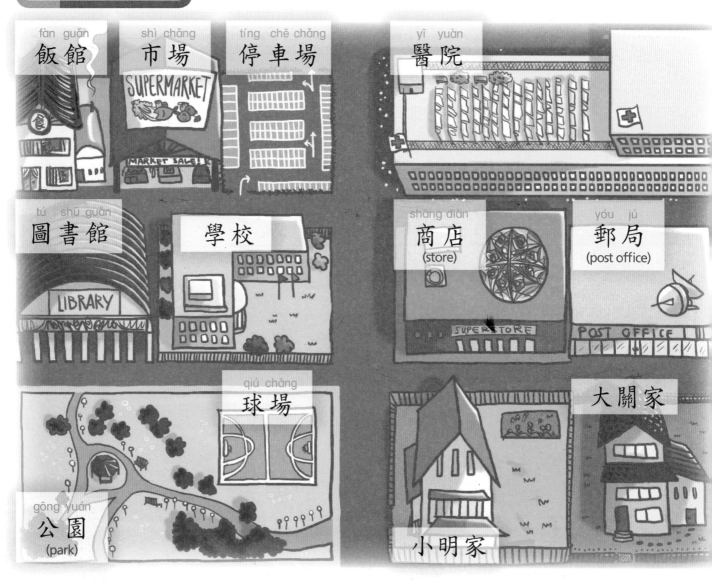

fàn guǎn
飯館

shì chǎng
市場

tíng chē chǎng
停車場

yī yuàn
醫院

SUPERMARKET

MARKET SALE!

tú shū guǎn
圖書館

學校

shāng diàn
商店
(store)

yóu jú
郵局
(post office)

LIBRARY

SUPERSTORE

POST OFFICE

qiú chǎng
球場

大關家

gōng yuán
公園
(park)

小明家

xiàng zuǒ zhuǎn
向左轉
(turn left)

xiàng qián zǒu
向前走
(go ahead)

xiàng yòu zhuǎn
向右轉
(turn right)

New Words

fàn guǎn 飯館 restaurant	shì chǎng 市場 market
tíng chē chǎng 停車場 parking lot	yī yuàn 醫院 hospital
tú shū guǎn 圖書館 library	qiú chǎng 球場 court for ball games (basketball, tennis, etc.)

 ## Mark the Route

Listen carefully to your teacher and trace out the route
on the map according to your teacher's directions.

xiàng zuǒ zhuǎn   tú shū guǎn
向左轉，圖書館。

xiàng qián   yī yuàn
向前走，是醫院。

shì chǎng   fù jìn
學校、市場在附近，

fāng biàn
做什麼，都方便。

TIP

mèng mǔ sān qiān
The Three Moves of Mencius' Mother (孟母三遷) is a traditional Chinese folklore which goes like this:

mèng zǐ
Mencius (孟子) was a great philosopher in ancient China, and one of the main followers of Confucius' ideas. Mencius did not like to study at all when he was a little boy. His mother strongly believed that the environment a child lived in was crucial to his development. Hence, she relocated their home from beside a cemetery to the side of a marketplace, and finally to a vicinity near a school.

If you could decide on a location to reside in, what would be the biggest consideration in your decision?

New Words

xiàng	zuǒ zhuǎn	xiàng qián	fù jìn	fāng biàn
向 towards	左轉 turn left	向前 forward	附近 nearby	方便 convenient

Let's Learn GRAMMAR

我家　後面　有　圖書館。
tú shū guǎn

學校附近有停車場。
fù jìn　tíng chē chǎng

我家對面有市場。
duì miàn　shì chǎng

圖書館　在　我家　後面。
tú shū guǎn

停車場在學校附近。
tíng chē chǎng　fù jìn

市場在我家對面。
shì chǎng　duì miàn

New Words

duì miàn
對面 opposite

zhù
住 live

TIP
"哪裡" and "什麼" are both interrogative pronouns. "哪裡" is used to ask about a location. When answering such a question, you simply need to replace "哪裡" with your answer without having to change the structure of the sentence.

……在哪裡？

Ⓐ：請問市場在哪裡？
shì chǎng

Ⓑ：市場在我家附近。
shì chǎng　fù jìn

Ⓐ：請問你住在哪裡？
zhù

Ⓑ：我住在圖書館後面。
zhù　tú shū guǎn

TIP

"到" in the sentence structure "從······到······" is a preposition which means "up to". However, "到" in the sentence "走路十分鐘就到了。" is a verb which means "to reach" or "to arrive at". In Examples 3 to 5, the speaker is aware of the travelling time between the two locations. To express the opinion that it does not take very long to travel to the destination, one can use the phrase "time + 就到了".

從······到······ (location)

從我家到市場要走十五分鐘。
shì chǎng

從學校到球場要走半個小時(hour)。
qiú chǎng   xiǎo shí

從我家到市場，走十五分鐘就到了。
shì chǎng

從學校到球場，走半個小時就到了。
qiú chǎng   xiǎo shí

從圖書館到醫院，開車二十分鐘就到了。
tú shū guǎn   yī yuàn

我　去　圖書館　看書。
tú shū guǎn

姑姑去停車場停車。
tíng chē chǎng tíng chē

外婆去市場買菜。
shì chǎng mǎi cài

New Words

tíng chē
停車 park (a vehicle)

mǎi cài
買菜 buy vegetables or groceries

WANT TO LEARN MORE?

Check out the Text > Sentence Pattern section in the Go300 CD.

Find a partner and practice the following dialogues.

New Words

lí 離	be away from
jìn 近	close, near
kàn bìng 看病	see a doctor

★ Task 1

Ⓐ：學校離你家近嗎？

Ⓑ：很近，學校就在我家對面。

Ⓐ：除了學校，你家附近還有什麼？

Ⓑ：我家附近還有圖書館、球場和飯館。

Ⓐ：你家附近什麼都有，真方便。

★ Task 2

Ⓐ：你家附近有醫院嗎？

Ⓑ：有。從我家到醫院，開車十分鐘就到了。
奶奶去醫院看病很方便。

Ⓐ：你家附近有市場嗎？

Ⓑ：我家附近沒有市場。從我家到最近的市場要
走四十五分鐘，我們得開車去買菜。

★ Task 3

Ⓐ 　_{tú shū guǎn}
請問圖書館怎麼走？

Ⓑ 　_{xiàng qián}　　　_{lù kǒu}　　_{xiàng zuǒ zhuǎn}
向前走，走到路口 (intersection) 向左轉，

　_{tú shū guǎn}
就可以到圖書館了。

Ⓐ 　　　_{tú shū guǎn}　_{qiú chǎng}
請問從圖書館到球場怎麼走？

Ⓑ 　　_{tú shū guǎn}　　　_{xiàng yòu zhuǎn}
從圖書館出來，向右轉，

　_{qiú chǎng}
就可以到球場了。

New Words

_{yòu zhuǎn}
右轉 turn right

★ Task 4

Ⓐ 我的筆壞了，學校
_{fù jìn} _{mài} _{shāng}
附近有賣 (sell) 筆的商
_{diàn}
店嗎？

Ⓑ 有，學校附近有賣
_{fù jìn} _{mài}
_{shāng diàn}
筆的商店。

Ⓐ 在學校的左邊，

還是右邊？

Ⓑ _{duì miàn}
在學校對面。

TIP

_{xiàng zuǒ zhuǎn}
Apart from "向左轉" (turn left) and
_{xiàng yòu zhuǎn}
"向右轉" (turn right), there are some regions in northern China such as Beijing where people
_{dōng}　　　_{xī}
commonly use "東" (east) , "西" (west),
_{nán}　　　　　_{běi}
"南" (south), and "北" (north) in giving directions. Intensive city planning in these cities since ancient times has given rise to neat and perpendicular roads, rendering it very convenient to give directions using the four
_{dōng xī nán běi}
cardinal directions (東西南北).

The compass, which is very useful in helping us find directions, is one of China's four main inventions. Even before the magnetic compass was invented, China had already invented a cart that worked on a gear system and always pointed south to help people find their directions.

The following dialogues are adapted from the Text > Dialogue section in your . Listen to the CD before reading the transcript on this page.

⭐ Task 5

Ⓐ : 你住在哪裡？
　　　zhù

Ⓑ : 我住在學校附近。
　　　zhù　　　　fù jìn

Ⓐ : 你家附近有什麼？
　　　　fù jìn

Ⓑ : 我家附近有學校、圖書館，還有市場。
　　　　fù jìn　　　　tú shū guǎn　　　shì chǎng

⭐ Task 6

Ⓐ : 我晚上給你打電話，方便嗎？
　　　　　　　　　　　fāng biàn

Ⓑ : 不要太晚，十點以後
　　　我就不可以接電話 (answer phone) 了。
　　　　　　　jiē diàn huà

⭐ Task 7

Ⓐ : 怎麼去你家？

Ⓑ : 從學校出來向左轉，走十分鐘就到了。
　　　　　　　xiàng zuǒ zhuǎn

Let's Learn CHARACTER

★ Linking Prepositions of Location

上　下　左　右

"上", "下", "左", and "右" are words that specifically describe a position. However, when they are placed together, the specificity decreases. For example, when paired together, "上下" and "左右" mean "approximately", and "上上下下" means "everywhere".

Ⓐ ： 你的學校有多少人？

Ⓑ ： 九百個上下。　　　　　　means "about 900 people"

Ⓒ ： 八百五十個左右。　　　　means "about 850 people"

我要找王醫生，可是醫院上上下下都找不到他。

★ Prepositions of Location that Look Similar

Some characters look very similar. Hence we have to be very careful when writing such characters so they will be differentiated. How can we remember the differentiation between these characters? Here, disassembling a character to its components is a good way to help us remember these characters, as illustrated by the example of "卡" below.

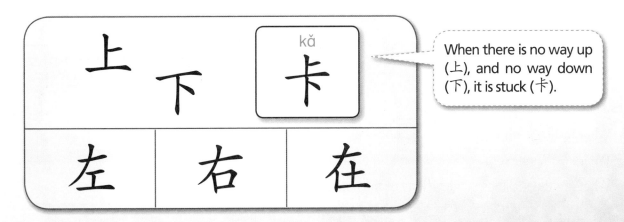

上　下　卡（kǎ）

左　右　在

When there is no way up (上), and no way down (下), it is stuck (卡).

Read the following text carefully.

我家前面有一個小學^{xiǎo xué}*，

我走五分鐘就到了；

我家後面有一個市^{shì chǎng}場，

媽媽買^{mǎi cài}菜很方^{fāng biàn}便；

我家左邊有一個醫^{yī yuàn}院，

奶奶可以走路去看^{kàn bìng}病；

圖^{tú shū guǎn}書館也在我家附^{fù jìn}近，

我們都愛去那^{nà lǐ}裡*看書。

* 小學 elementary school

* 那裡 there

Answer these questions in Chinese.

1 What facility is on the left of the author's house?

2 Where is the marketplace in relation to the author's house?

3 What are the facilities in the vicinity of the author's house?

Text 2

Read the following text carefully.

去年八月，我們一家人去了
台北*看*舅舅。
tái bě kàn

到了台北，爸爸問我們：「怎麼去舅舅家？」
tái bě

姊姊說：「我們可以看地圖*。」
dì tú

哥哥說：「我可以用電腦找到舅舅家。」

弟弟說：「我們可以請舅舅來接我們。」弟弟
說完，我們就看到舅舅來接我們了。

我們在台北住了兩天，我們去了圖書館看書，
tái bě tú shū guǎn
還去了市場買菜。台北是一個很大的城市*，也是一
shì chǎng mǎi cài tái bě chéng shì
個很好玩的城市。
chéng shì

*台北 Taipei   *看 visit   *地圖 map   *城市 city

Answer these questions in Chinese.

1   Where did the author go during his school break in August?

2   The author's siblings suggested a few ways to get to their uncle's house. What are they? Do you have any other suggestions?

3   Which places did the author visit when he was in Shanghai?

How can I get there?

1 Pair up and obtain a dice. Take turns to role-play A and B.

2 Toss the dice twice—the first one is to determine A's present location and the second is to determine his next destination.

3 Refer to the map on page 52 of this book and carry out the dialogue below. The words in red may be replaced accordingly.

圖書館 *tú shū guǎn*

市場 *shì chǎng*

球場 *qiú chǎng*

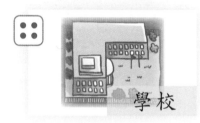
學校 *xué xiào*

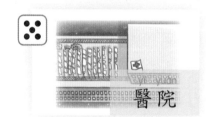
醫院 *yī yuàn*

小明家 *xiǎo míng jiā*

Ⓐ：我在球場，請問市場怎麼走？
（*qiú chǎng*）（*shì chǎng*）

Ⓑ：從球場出來，向右轉，到了路口向左轉，看到停車場
（*qiú chǎng*）（*xiàng yòu zhuǎn*）（*lù kǒu xiàng zuǒ zhuǎn*）（*tíng chē chǎng*）
向左轉，就可以到市場了。
（*xiàng zuǒ zhuǎn*）（*shì chǎng*）

I can...	Excellent 😊	Good 🙂	Fair 😐	Needs Improvement 🙁
1 ask for directions using "……在哪裡？" and "……怎麼走？".	☐	☐	☐	☐
2 give directions to a location in the neighborhood, and estimate the time needed to get there.	☐	☐	☐	☐
3 describe the facilities in the vicinity of an area.	☐	☐	☐	☐
4 understand the meaning when prepositions of location are paired or grouped together such as "上下", "左右", and "上上下下".	☐	☐	☐	☐
5 write "住", "向", "轉", "圖", and "館".	☐	☐	☐	☐

LEARNING LOG

我的心情
My Moods

My Goals

1. Express my emotions and moods
2. Explain the cause of or reason for something
3. Recognize that radicals may appear in various positions in different characters
4. Become familiar with vocabulary associated with emotions and moods

Get Started

kāi xīn
開心

xiào
笑
(laugh)

nán guò
難過

hài pà
害怕
(scared)

Play It

1 Students discuss with their teacher and decide on accompanying facial expressions or actions for the vocabulary on this page.

2 Play "Simon says …": the teacher chooses a word from this page and says it aloud in Chinese. If the teacher says "Simon says …" before that word, students have to perform the associated facial expression or action. If the teacher does not say "Simon says …" before the word, students have to maintain the previous facial expression or action.

kū
哭
(cry)

chǎo jià
吵架

dǎ jià
打架

shēng qì
生氣

New Words

kāi xīn	nán guò	chǎo jià	dǎ jià	shēng qì
開心 happy	難過 sad	吵架 quarrel	打架 fight	生氣 angry

Let's CHANT (Go 300)

xīn qíng   měi lì
心情好，看人看花都美麗，

xīn qíng   nán kàn
心情壞，看人看花都難看。

chǎo jià mà rén
吵架罵人沒有用，

zì jǐ shēng qì   nán guò
自己生氣又難過。

TIP In Chinese culture, it is expected of one to hide any feelings of animosity and be cordial to one another. To maintain harmony, the Chinese would generally bottle up their feelings rather than face any confrontation or conflict.

When you feel angry about something, how do you express your emotions?

New Words

xīn qíng	měi lì	nán kàn	mà rén	zì jǐ
心情 mood	美麗 beautiful	難看 terrible, ugly	罵人 scold	自己 self

我的心情 65

TIP

The phrase "自己" (self) refers to the subject of each clause.

zì jǐ
自己

zì jǐ
我自己會做飯，會洗衣服。

"自己" in this sentence refers to "me".

zì jǐ　　　　zì jǐ
自己的作業要自己寫。

"自己" in this sentence has no particular reference; it refers to anybody who hears this sentence.

　　　　　dài　　　　　　　　　zì jǐ
哥哥不帶弟弟去打球，弟弟就自己去了。

"自己" in this sentence refers to "弟弟".

yīn wèi　　　　　　　　suǒ yǐ
因為　我生病了，　所以　我沒去上學。

yīn wèi　　　　　　　dǎ jià　　suǒ yǐ　　　mà
因為堂哥和同學打架，所以叔叔罵他。

　　　　wèi shén me xīn qíng
Ⓐ：你們為什麼心情不好？

　　yīn wèi
Ⓑ：因為我找不到我要的書，
　　suǒ yǐ　　xīn qíng
　　所以我心情不好。

　　xīn qíng　　　　　yīn wèi
Ⓒ：我心情不好，因為我不能
　　參加球隊。

TIP

"因為……，所以……" is a sentence structure that expresses cause and effect. The phrase after "因為" conveys the cause and the phrase after "所以" conveys the effect. When the effect is positioned at the beginning of the sentence, the word "所以" may be omitted, leaving "因為" to introduce the cause in the second clause.

New Words

dài	yīn wèi	suǒ yǐ	wèi shén me
帶 bring	因為 because	所以 so	為什麼 why, what for

你 　為什麼　 心情不好？
wèi shén me　xīn qíng

她為什麼考得不好？
wèi shén me

他為什麼不來打球？
wèi shén me

為什麼　 你　 心情不好？
wèi shén me　　xīn qíng

為什麼她考得不好？
wèi shén me

為什麼他不來打球？
wèi shén me

TIP

The question tag "為什麼" may be used to ask for a reason or a motive. It can be positioned before or after the subject, or at the end of the question.

Questions with "為什麼" can often be answered with the "因為……，所以……" sentence structure.

"為什麼 + 不" is often a question in retort, indicating that the speaker feels the situation should have been feasible or possible.

你　 心情不好，　 為什麼？
xīn qíng　　　wèi shén me

她考得不好，為什麼？
wèi shén me

他不來打球，為什麼？
wèi shén me

Go300

WANT TO LEARN MORE?

Check out the Text > Sentence Pattern section in the Go300 CD.

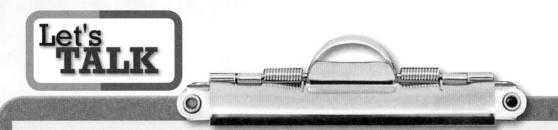

Find a partner and practice the following dialogues.

Task 1

Ⓐ 你會和同學吵架^{chǎo jià}嗎？

Ⓑ 我們很少^{hěn shǎo} (seldom) 吵架^{chǎo jià}，因為吵架^{yīn wèi chǎo jià}沒有用。

Ⓐ 你的成績不好，你媽媽會罵^{mà}你嗎？

Ⓑ 不會。媽媽說：「成績好壞不重要，用心做好最重要。」

Task 2

Ⓐ 你怎麼了？

Ⓑ 我心情^{xīn qíng}不好。

Ⓐ 為什麼^{wèi shén me}？

Ⓑ 因為^{yīn wèi}我吃了哥哥的麵包，哥哥很生氣^{shēng qì}。

Ⓐ 你對哥哥說對不起，再買一個麵包給他，你哥哥就不會生氣^{shēng qì}了。

★ Task 3

Ⓐ : 我看你很開心。
_{kāi xīn}

Ⓑ : 因為我心情好。
_{yīn wèi　xīn qíng}

Ⓐ : 為什麼你心情好？
_{wèi shén me　　xīn qíng}

Ⓑ : 因為我找到心情好的方法 (method)。
_{yīn wèi　　　　xīn qíng　　fāng fǎ}
多笑心情就好，少生氣心情也好。
_{xiào xīn qíng　　　shēng qì xīn qíng}

Ⓐ : 所以我們要多笑，少生氣。
_{suǒ yǐ　　　　xiào　　shēng qì}

★ Task 4

Ⓐ : 你今天心情好嗎？
_{xīn qíng}

Ⓑ : _____ 。

Ⓐ : 你為什麼 _____ ？
_{wèi shén me}

Ⓑ : _____ 。

Task 5

Can you identify the pairs of dialogue from the eight utterances below? Organize them into four dialogues and fill in the following table. When this is done, you may listen to the Text > Dialogue section in your [Go300] for the correct answers and fill in the blanks.

①	A:	②	A:	③	A:	④	A:
	B:		B:		B:		B:

① 他們兩個都要這個_____，所以吵架了。 <small>suǒ yǐ chǎo jià</small>

② 你在罵誰？ <small>mà</small>

③ 我考得不好，所以很_____。 <small>suǒ yǐ</small>

④ 你為什麼心情不好？ <small>wèi shén me xīn qíng</small>

⑤ 外婆愛_____，我們可以買花去看她。

⑥ 我在罵弟弟，_____。 <small>mà</small>

⑦ 他們兩個在吵什麼？ <small>chǎo</small>

⑧ 去醫院看外婆，要帶什麼？ <small>dài</small>

Let's Learn RADICAL

We have learnt that radicals bear meanings and classify characters into various semantic categories. For example, a character with the radical "女" is associated with the meaning of femininity; a character with the radical "言" is related to speech. However, the position of a radical in each character varies—it may be positioned as the top, bottom, left, or right component. This lesson illustrates the different positions of some radicals.

 **Trace It**

Trace out the radical of the last character in each category using a color pencil or highlighter.

Radicals in the top component

Radicals in the bottom component

Radicals in the left component

Radicals in the right component

 **Text** 1 **Go 300**

Read the following text carefully.

天[*]，有好天氣，壞天氣，
（tiān）

人，有好心情，壞心情。
（xīn qíng）（xīn qíng）

天，不是天天好天氣，
（tiān）

人，不是天天好心情。
（xīn qíng）

天氣不好，我在家裡不出去，

心情不好，我就出去走一走。
（xīn qíng）

明天，又是好天氣，

明天，又是好心情。
（xīn qíng）

* 天 sky

Answer these questions in Chinese.

1 What does the author do when he is in a good mood?

2 What does he do when he is in a bad mood?

3 At times, the weather may be pleasant or dreadful; moods may
   be good or bad. Are your moods influenced by the weather?

Read the following text carefully.

　　姊姊和表妹要參加學校樂隊，媽媽買了一樣的白衣服給她們。

　　姊姊瘦瘦的，穿上白衣服很好看；表妹胖胖的，穿上白衣服也很好看。可是姊姊不愛自己(zì jǐ)的樣子，她說自己(zì jǐ)太瘦了；表妹也不愛自己(zì jǐ)的樣子，她說自己(zì jǐ)太胖了。

　　媽媽說：「一個人胖一點兒，瘦一點兒沒關係，外表(wài biǎo)*好不好看不重要，心裡(xīn lǐ)*美(měi)*最重要。你的心裡(xīn lǐ)美(měi)，大家看你都好看。」

*外表 appearance　*心裡 one's heart and mind　*美 beautiful

Answer these questions in Chinese.

1　Why does the author's mother buy his sister and cousin a set of white outfit each?

2　Do the author's sister and cousin like how they look respectively? Why?

3　Do you think one's outward appearance and beauty are important? Why?

"North–South–East–West" Origami Game

1 Prepare a square piece of paper for a game of origami.

(1) Fold the paper in half diagonally. Fold it again in half. Open it and fold in each corner to meet at the center of the paper (see diagram ❶).

(2) Flip the paper over on its back and fold in each corner to meet at the center of the paper (see diagram ❷).

(3) On the side of the paper which looks like the character "田", write the four emotions ("生氣", "開心", "難過", and "害怕") in the four squares (see diagram ❸).

(4) Flip the paper over and in each triangle, write the possible reasons for the feelings reflected on the other side. Write down two reasons for each emotion (see diagram ❹).

(5) Fold the paper into a rectangle to create a flexagon (see diagram ❺).

❶ 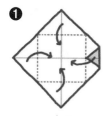 ❷ 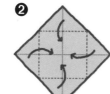 ❸ 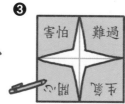 ❹ 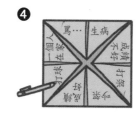 ❺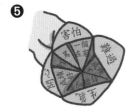

2 Find a classmate and ask him to select any of the four emotions you have written down and a number from 1 to 10. According to the number selected by your classmate, flex your flexagon vertically and then horizontally to reveal the reason for the feeling. With the sentence structure "因為……，所以……", your classmate has to read out the entire sentence. For example, "因為我大考的成績好，所以我很開心。"

3 Play this game with five other classmates. On a separate sheet of paper, write down their sentences and obtain their signatures.

LEARNING LOG

I can...	Excellent	Good	Fair	Needs Improvement
1 use vocabulary associated with emotions to express my moods.	☐	☐	☐	☐
2 identify who the phrase "自己" refers to in different sentences and use it appropriately.	☐	☐	☐	☐
3 use "為什麼……?" to ask for a reason, and "因為……，所以……" to give a reason.	☐	☐	☐	☐
4 recognize that radicals may appear in the top, bottom, left, or right component in different characters.	☐	☐	☐	☐
5 write "情", "美", "吵", "因", and "為".	☐	☐	☐	☐

我看球賽
Watching a Ball Game

My Goals

1 Describe the happenings at a ball game
2 Make comparisons between two subjects
3 Understand how the pronunciation of some characters is determined by its components
4 Become familiar with vocabulary associated with ball games and the feelings associated with watching the games

bàng qiú
棒球

lán qiú
籃球

zú qiú
足球
(soccer)

zhuō qiú   pīng pāng qiú
桌球/乒乓球

wǎng qiú
網球
(tennis)

měi shì zú qiú
美式足球
(American Football)

bǐ sài
比賽

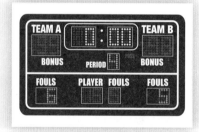

duì yíng
A 隊 贏

duì shū
B 隊 輸

Work It Out

1 What are the different scoring systems of ball games? How is the champion determined in various ball games?

2 What ball games have similar scoring systems?

Discuss the above questions with a friend or research on it on the Internet, and present the information in the following class.

New Words

bàng qiú 棒球 baseball	lán qiú 籃球 basketball	zhuō qiú pīng pāng qiú 桌球/乒乓球 table tennis

bǐ sài
比賽 contest   ·····隊 team ...   yíng 贏 win   shū 輸 lose

bàng qiú　　　　zhuō qiú
打棒球，打桌球，

jīng cǎi qiú sài　　　jǐn zhāng
精彩球賽真緊張，

你一球，我一球，

yíng　　shū
你贏我輸沒關係。

New Words

jīng cǎi
精彩 outstanding, fantastic

qiú sài
球賽 ball game

jǐn zhāng
緊張 nervous

TIP
In ancient China, archery was viewed as a competition between noblemen. It was standard procedure for opponents to bow to each other before entering the competition grounds. A round of drinks and merry-making would also take place after the competition regardless of the results of the contest to show the men's chivalry and sportsmanship.

Qualities of a sportsman (respecting one's opponents, doing one's best, not gloating after a victory and not disheartened after a loss) have transcended time and remain unchanged today.

What is the most important thing to you in a competition? Have you ever lost in a competition and yet felt very satisfied and proud of yourself?

TIP
"桌球" has different meanings in different regions. In northern China, it refers to billiards; in southern China, it refers to table tennis.

bǐ
比

	1	2	3	4	5	6	7	8	9	
紅隊	0	0	0	2	3	2	0	2	1	10
藍隊	0	0	1	2	0	2	0	0	2	7

十比七，紅隊贏，藍隊輸。

紅隊贏了三分，藍隊輸了三分。

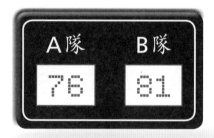

七十六比八十一，B隊贏了，贏了五分。

B隊贏A隊五分。

十一比九，大關輸了，輸了兩分。

大關輸小明兩分。

New Words

bǐ	
比 compare	
fēn	
分 score	

我 比(bǐ) 表弟 大兩歲。

"我比表弟大兩歲。"
means the same as
"我大表弟兩歲。".

哥哥比(bǐ)我高。

媽媽比(bǐ)爸爸緊張(jǐn zhāng)。

奶奶比(bǐ)我難過。

這本書比(bǐ)那本書便宜。

小明的成績比(bǐ)我的好。

下午的球賽(qiú sài)比(bǐ)上午的精彩(jīng cǎi)。

比(bǐ)一比(bǐ)

我們來比(bǐ)一比(bǐ)，看誰打得好。

我們兩個比(bǐ)一比(bǐ)，看誰寫得好。

小明喜歡(xǐ huān)和同學比(bǐ)一比(bǐ)，看誰考得好。

New Words

喜歡(xǐ huān) like

Go300

WANT TO LEARN MORE?

Check out the Text > Sentence Pattern section in the Go300 CD.

Find a partner and practice the following dialogues.

⭐ Task 1

Ⓐ : 今天我看了一場很精彩的球賽。
　　　　　　chǎng　jīng cǎi　　qiú sài

Ⓑ : 今天是哪一隊和哪一隊的比賽？
　　　　　　duì　　　　　duì　bǐ sài

Ⓐ : 今天是紅隊和綠隊的籃球比賽。
　　　　　　duì　　　duì　lán qiú bǐ sài
　　　兩隊你一球，我一球，打得很精彩。
　　　duì　　　　　　　　　　　　　jīng cǎi

⭐ Task 2

Ⓐ : 今天下午是哪一隊和哪一隊的比賽？
　　　　　　　　　duì　　　　　　duì　bǐ sài

Ⓑ : 今天下午是_____和_____的比賽。
　　　　　　　　　　　　　　　　　　　　　bǐ sài

Ⓐ : 哪一個隊贏了？
　　　　　　duì yíng

Ⓑ : _____。

Ⓐ : _____隊輸了幾分？
　　　duì shū　　fēn

Ⓑ : _____。

Task 3

Ⓐ： 你喜歡什麼運動？

Ⓑ： 我喜歡打球，我最喜歡打棒球，也喜歡看球賽。

Ⓐ： 你喜歡看哪一隊的比賽？

Ⓑ： 我喜歡看＿＿＿＿隊的比賽。你要不要一起去看球賽？

Ⓐ： 我想去看球賽，可是球賽的票太貴了，

＿＿＿＿＿＿＿＿＿＿＿＿＿。

Task 4

Ⓐ： 明天學校要大考。

Ⓑ： 明天你要考什麼？

Ⓐ： 明天我要考中文。我要和小明比一比，看誰考得好。

Ⓑ： 你緊張嗎？

Ⓐ： 我有一點兒緊張，可是我媽媽比我還緊張。

New Words

yùn dòng 運 動 exercise	piào 票 ticket

The following dialogues are adapted from the Text > Dialogue section in your  Go 300 . Listen to the CD
before reading the transcript on this page.

⭐Task 5

Ⓐ : 你要去看球賽嗎？
　　　　　　qiú　sài

Ⓑ : 不去，我的功課還沒有做完。

⭐Task 6

Ⓐ : 球賽一張票多少錢？
　　qiú　sài　　　piào

Ⓑ : 一張票六十塊錢，一張學生票
　　　　piào　　　　　　　　　　　　　　piào

　　三十塊錢。

⭐Task 7

Ⓐ : 比賽精彩嗎？哪一個球隊贏了？哪一個球隊輸了？
　　bǐ　sài　jīng cǎi　　　　　　　qiú　duì　yíng　　　　　　qiú　duì　shū

Ⓑ : 很精彩！藍隊贏了，綠隊輸了。
　　　jīng cǎi　　　duì　yíng　　　duì　shū

⭐Task 8

Ⓐ : 你喜歡打什麼球？
　　　xǐ　huān

Ⓑ : ＿＿＿＿＿＿＿＿＿＿＿＿＿＿

Let's Learn CHARACTER

Some characters in Chinese are made up of a single component; others are composed of a combination of different components. Some components classify characters into various semantic categories, as we have learnt of the radicals "女", "言", and "心". Some components can also determine the pronunciation of the characters they are part of. In the following lesson, we introduce a component that can determine the pronunciation of its character.

qīng

青

"青" literally means the color "green". It also connotes the meaning of "beauty" and "happiness". When "青" is part of a character, the character is often semantically associated with joyful events. The pronunciation of the characters with "青" are also similar.

Practice It

Write down the *pinyin* of the following characters.

精

晴

情

請

晴

"晴" means "a fine day". This character will appear in page 112 of this book. Have a guess at pronouncing this character before checking out the correct pronunciation.

Text 1

Read the following text carefully.

哥哥參加學校的球隊，下星期六要比^{bǐ sài}賽，爸爸

要我算一算，我們一共要買幾張票^{piào}？

我算一算：爺爺、奶奶、外公、外婆、姑媽^{gū mā}*

一家四個人、叔叔一家三個人、舅舅一家五個人、

姨媽一家兩個人，加上^{jiā shàng}*爸爸、媽媽、姊姊，還有我，

一共二十二個人，要買二十二張票^{piào}。

一張票^{piào}三塊錢，一共多少錢？

* 姑媽 aunt (father's sister)

* 加上 add

Answer these questions in Chinese.

1　What tickets is the author buying?

2　How many people are there in his paternal aunt's family?

3　How many people are there in the author's family? How much will all the tickets cost?

4　Read the passage in the CD (Text > Reading: 1-2). Who in the author's family is not able to go to the game? How many tickets does the author buy eventually, and what is the total cost of the tickets?

Read the following text carefully.

哥哥星期六要比<ruby>賽<rt>bǐ sài</rt></ruby>了，媽媽<ruby>比<rt>bǐ</rt></ruby>哥哥還<ruby>緊張<rt>jǐn zhāng</rt></ruby>，要

他多喝水，多吃<ruby>水果<rt>shuǐ guǒ</rt></ruby>*，多休息，不要玩電腦遊戲。

<ruby>比賽<rt>bǐ sài</rt></ruby>那天，哥哥打得很好，可是，他們<ruby>球隊<rt>qiú duì</rt></ruby>

<ruby>輸<rt>shū</rt></ruby>了，<ruby>輸<rt>shū</rt></ruby>了兩<ruby>分<rt>fēn</rt></ruby>，哥哥很難過。爸爸說：「<ruby>輸<rt>shū</rt></ruby>了

沒關係，你打得很好。」

我說：「哥哥打得很<ruby>棒<rt>bàng</rt></ruby>*！哥哥打得很<ruby>精彩<rt>jīng cǎi</rt></ruby>！」

我們都<ruby>喜歡<rt>xǐ huān</rt></ruby>看他打球。

*水果 fruit   *棒 great

Answer these questions in Chinese.

1   Who is playing in the game? Who is the most nervous about it?

2   Does Older Brother win or lose his game? How does he feel?

3   What does Father say to Older Brother after the game?

Go 300

WANT TO LEARN MORE?

Check out the Text > Reading section in the Go300 CD.

Telephone Invitation To A Ball Game

1 Pair up with a partner and assume roles of A and B.

2 Obtain a dice and B tosses it twice.

3 The number from the first toss determines the ball game that B would like to watch: 1 or 2 – Table Tennis Game; 3 or 4 – Baseball Game; 5 or 6 – Soccer Game.

4 The number obtained from the second toss determines how much money B has: 1 – $10, 2 – $20, and so on.

5 Change the details of the following conversation according to the information determined from tossing the dice, bearing in mind proper phone etiquette.

Ⓐ：你想看<ruby>球賽<rt>qiú sài</rt></ruby>嗎？

Ⓑ：我<ruby>喜歡<rt>xǐ huān</rt></ruby>看<ruby>足球比賽<rt>zú qiú bǐ sài</rt></ruby>。什麼時候有<ruby>足球比賽<rt>zú qiú bǐ sài</rt></ruby>？
一張<ruby>票<rt>piào</rt></ruby>多少錢？

Ⓐ：十一月十七日有<ruby>足球比賽<rt>zú qiú bǐ sài</rt></ruby>，一張<ruby>票<rt>piào</rt></ruby>三十五塊錢。

Ⓑ：我有六十塊錢，我可以和你一起去看。／
<ruby>票<rt>piào</rt></ruby>太貴了，我不能去。

I can...	Excellent	Good	Fair	Needs Improvement
1 name common sports such as baseball, table tennis and soccer in Chinese.	☐	☐	☐	☐
2 use sports-related vocabulary such as "OO比OO", "精彩", "輸贏", and "緊張" to describe a game or one's feelings when watching a game.	☐	☐	☐	☐
3 use "比" to make a comparison.	☐	☐	☐	☐
4 recognize that characters with the component "青" are often associated with the meaning of beauty and happiness.	☐	☐	☐	☐
5 write "精", "彩", "運", "票", and "比".	☐	☐	☐	☐

LEARNING LOG

我的愛好
My Hobbies

My Goals

1 Talk about my hobbies and ask others about their hobbies
2 Describe the frequency in the occurrence of an action
3 Describe two simultaneous actions in the same sentence
4 Recognize some Chinese characters with two or more forms of pronunciation
5 Become familiar with vocabulary associated with one's hobbies

Get Started

chàng gē
唱 歌

tiào wǔ
跳 舞

yīn yuè
聽 音 樂
(listen to music)

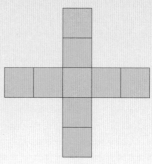

看 書

huà huà
畫 畫
(paint)

shū fǎ
書 法
(calligraphy)

pǎo bù
跑 步

liáo tiān
聊 天
(chat)

diàn yǐng
看 電 影
(watch a movie)

Play It

1 Draw nine boxes to make up a cross-grid puzzle (see diagram below). In any order you wish, fill in each box with one of the nine words or phrases introduced on this page.

2 The teacher will recite the vocabulary in any order she wishes. Students circle the vocabulary in their cross-grid puzzle as they are read out. The first student to circle all the vocabulary in a straight line wins.

3 Alternatively, the teacher may draw lots to select a student who will read aloud a word or phrase from this page. An accurate pronunciation entitles him to circle that word or phrase in his cross-grid puzzle. A wrong pronunciation will relegate the turn to another student.

New Words

chàng gē	tiào wǔ	yīn yuè	pǎo bù
唱歌 sing a song	跳舞 dance	音樂 music	跑步 run, jog

Let's CHANT　Go300

每個人都有愛^{ài}好^{hào}，

你愛打球愛運動，

她愛唱^{chàng}歌^{gē}愛跳^{tiào}舞^{wǔ}，

我愛看書玩電腦。

New Words

愛^{ài}好^{hào} hobby

Let's Learn GRAMMAR

cháng cháng
常常

cháng cháng péng yǒu chàng gē
姊姊常常和朋友一起唱歌。

tiào wǔ cháng cháng
表妹喜歡跳舞,她常常參加

tiào wǔ
跳舞比賽。

cì
大關每個星期來我家兩次,

cháng cháng
他常常來找哥哥。

TIP

"很少","有時","常常", and "每次" are time adverbials which indicate the frequency of an action or event. "每次" means "every time"; "常常" means "often"; "有時" means "sometimes"; and "很少" means "seldom". In a typical sentence structure, they are positioned before the verb phrase.

For example:
➤ 我家附近有圖書館和球場,我有時去看書,有時去打球。
➤ 小明一年去一次奶奶家,他很少去看奶奶。

姊姊	yì biān 一邊	走路,	yì biān 一邊	chàng gē 唱歌。

yì biān yì biān
哥哥一邊看球賽,一邊喝果汁。

yì biān yīn yuè yì biān
妹妹一邊聽音樂,一邊掃落葉。

yì biān yì biān
媽媽一邊做飯,一邊打電話。

New Words

cháng cháng 常常 often	péng yǒu 朋友 friend	cì 次 time; instance	yì biān 一邊……,yì biān 一邊…… do the things at the same time

Expansion of Phrases
AB ➔ A...B

上課 ➔ 上什麼課？

chàng gē
唱歌 ➔ 唱什麼歌？
chàng   gē

tiào wǔ
跳舞 ➔ 跳什麼舞？
tiào   wǔ

打球 ➔ 打什麼球？

TIP   Some characters may be combined to form meaningful phrases. They may even be separated in a sentence and yet retain their meaning as when they are combined.

老師上的課很有用。

chàng   gē
弟弟唱的歌很好聽。

tiào   wǔ
堂哥跳的舞很好看。

měi cì
我每次都上五十分鐘的課。

měi cì   xiǎo shí
哥哥每次都打一個小時的球。

měi cì   tiào   wǔ
姊姊每次都跳三十分鐘的舞。

New Words

měi cì
每次 every time

xiǎo shí
小時 hour

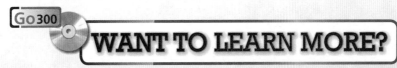

Go300

WANT TO LEARN MORE?

Check out the Text > Sentence Pattern section in the Go300 CD.

Find a partner and practice the following dialogues.

⭐ Task 1

Ⓐ：
<ruby>愛好<rt>ài hào</rt></ruby>
你的愛好是什麼？

Ⓑ：
<ruby>音樂<rt>yīn yuè</rt></ruby> <ruby>愛好<rt>ài hào</rt></ruby>
我喜歡聽音樂。你的愛好是什麼？

Ⓐ：
<ruby>唱歌<rt>chàng gē</rt></ruby> <ruby>音樂<rt>yīn yuè</rt></ruby>
我喜歡唱歌。你什麼時候聽音樂？

Ⓑ：
<ruby>常常一邊<rt>cháng cháng yì biān</rt></ruby> <ruby>一邊<rt>yì biān</rt></ruby> <ruby>音樂<rt>yīn yuè</rt></ruby>
我常常一邊寫作業，一邊聽音樂。

<ruby>唱歌<rt>chàng gē</rt></ruby>
你什麼時候唱歌？

Ⓐ：
<ruby>常常一邊掃地<rt>cháng cháng yì biān sǎo dì</rt></ruby>
我常常一邊掃地 (sweep the floor)，

<ruby>一邊唱歌<rt>yì biān chàng gē</rt></ruby>
一邊唱歌。

⭐ Task 2

Ⓐ：
星期天你要做什麼？

Ⓑ：
<ruby>跳舞<rt>tiào wǔ</rt></ruby>
星期天我要去跳舞。

Ⓐ：
<ruby>每次<rt>měi cì</rt></ruby> <ruby>跳<rt>tiào</rt></ruby> <ruby>小時<rt>xiǎo shí</rt></ruby>
每次要跳幾個小時？

Ⓑ：
<ruby>每次<rt>měi cì</rt></ruby> <ruby>跳<rt>tiào</rt></ruby> <ruby>小時<rt>xiǎo shí</rt></ruby> <ruby>舞<rt>wǔ</rt></ruby>
我每次都跳三個小時的舞。

Ⓐ：
<ruby>跳舞<rt>tiào wǔ</rt></ruby> <ruby>跳舞<rt>tiào wǔ</rt></ruby>
我也喜歡跳舞，跳舞很開心。

⭐Task 3

Ⓐ : 你和朋友有一樣的愛好嗎？
　　　　　　　péng yǒu　　　　　　　　ài hào

Ⓑ : 有，我們都愛運動，我們常常一起運動。
　　　　　　　　　　　　　　　cháng cháng

Ⓐ : 你和朋友會吵架嗎？
　　　　péng yǒu

Ⓑ : 我們很少 (seldom) 吵架，因為吵架沒有用。
　　　　hěn shǎo

⭐Task 4

Ⓐ : 你喜歡運動嗎？

Ⓑ : 喜歡。

Ⓐ : 你喜歡做什麼運動？

Ⓑ : 我喜歡跳舞，我和妹妹明天要參加跳舞比賽。
　　　　tiào wǔ　　　　　　　　　　　　　　tiào wǔ

Ⓐ : 你們參加比賽緊張嗎？

Ⓑ : 我不緊張，可是妹妹很緊張。

The following dialogues can be found in the Text > Dialogue section in your ⊙ Go300 . Listen to the CD first before practicing the dialogues in pairs. The student assuming the role of B has to complete the dialogues using his own information.

★ Task 5

Ⓐ : 你的愛好是什麼？
　　　ài hào

Ⓑ : （我喜歡聽音樂，也喜歡跳舞。）
　　　　　yīn yuè　　　　　　　　tiào wǔ

Ⓐ : 你喜歡聽什麼音樂？
　　　　　　　　yīn yuè

Ⓑ : _____ 。

★ Task 6

Ⓐ : 你在學什麼？

Ⓑ : （我在學跳舞。）
　　　　　tiào wǔ

Ⓐ : 每次學幾個小時？
　　　měi cì　　　xiǎo shí

Ⓑ : _____ 。

Let's Learn CHARACTER

Some Chinese characters have more than one form of pronunciation and the variants typically have different meanings. The following illustrates some of these words that we have learnt before.

好
hǎo 弟弟上課很用心，他的成績很好。
hào 我的愛好是跳舞，我喜歡一邊唱歌，
    ài hào *tiào wǔ*   *yì biān chàng gē*
    yì biān tiào wǔ
    一邊跳舞。

便
pián 這本書三塊錢，很便宜。
biàn 圖書館在我家對面，很方便。

得
de 昨天的球賽打得很精彩。
děi 我明天得上課，還得參加唱歌比賽。
                      chàng gē

A third way of pronouncing "得" is dé, which means "obtain or achieve".

⭐ Practice It

Fill in the *pinyin* on top of the boxed characters.

① 妹妹的 | 愛好 | 是唱歌，她唱 | 得 | 真 | 好聽 |。
                chàng gē   *chàng*

② 從學校到我家 | 得 | 開車半個小時，很不 | 方便 |。
                    xiǎo shí

Let's READ

Text 1

Read the following text carefully.

dòng dòng
每天都要動*一動，

dòng dòng nǎo
動動腦*，看書、上學、想問題；

dòng dòng   jiā shì
動動手，打球、打字、做家事*；

dòng dòng   chàng gē
動動嘴，吃喝、唱歌、打電話；

dòng dòng jiǎo   pǎo bù   tiào tiào wǔ
動動腳*，散步、跑步、跳跳舞。

dòng   dòng   dòng jiǎo
動嘴、動手又動腳，不要忘了多

dòng nǎo
動腦。

* 動 exercise; to move something
* 腦 brain   * 家事 chores   * 腳 foot

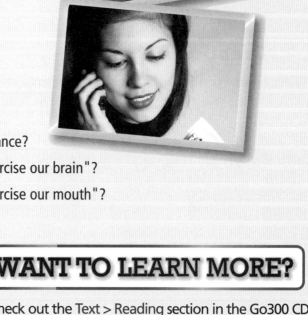

Answer these questions in Chinese.

1 How do we exercise when we take a stroll, jog, or dance?

2 According to the text, what do we do when we "exercise our brain"?

3 According to the text, what do we do when we "exercise our mouth"?

WANT TO LEARN MORE?

Check out the Text > Reading section in the Go300 CD.

Read the following text carefully.

每個人都有愛好，爺爺愛看書，奶奶愛散步。

爸爸的愛好是和朋友聊天，媽媽的愛好是種花。

妹妹喜歡跳舞，姊姊愛買衣服，我喜歡一邊聽音樂，一邊唱歌。

哥哥的愛好是看書，他喜歡去圖書館看很多不同的書，因為他想做醫生。

媽媽說：「做自己喜歡的事，心情就會好，所以每一個人都要有自己的愛好。」

Answer these questions in Chinese.

1 What does everyone in the author's family like to do? Write down each of their hobbies in Chinese in the table below.

爺爺	奶奶	爸爸	媽媽

哥哥	姊姊	我 (the author)	妹妹

2 What is Older Brother's ambition?

3 Why should all of us have a hobby that we enjoy?

Let's DO IT

1. Obtain a blank piece of paper and a rubber band. Fold the paper into eight equal parts and cut out eight identical strips of paper. Stack the eight strips of paper together, fold them in the middle and secure the middle with the rubber band to create a booklet (See diagram ❶ and ❷).

2. Write down "1. 愛好" on the front cover, and "2. 去哪裡？" on the back cover. Flip the booklet onto the reverse side so that its middle pages now become the front and back covers. Write down "3. 和什麼人？" on this front cover and "4. 常去嗎？" on this back cover (See diagram ❸ and ❹).

3. In every page in the booklet, write down the possible answers to the prompts provided on the cover pages. For example, (1) 跳舞；(2) 學校；(3) 朋友；(4) 常常.

4. Get five friends for this activity. Draw lots to choose the phrases from the booklet and practice the dialogues with Ⓐ 's questions as provided below. Ⓑ should answers accordingly and in complete sentences.

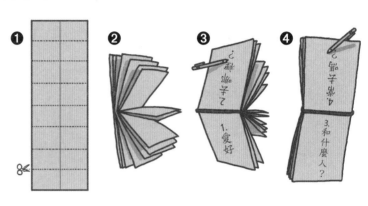

Ⓐ：你的愛好是什麼？
<small>ài hào</small>

Ⓐ：你去哪裡跳舞？
<small>tiào wǔ</small>

Ⓐ：你和誰一起去學校跳舞？
<small>tiào wǔ</small>

Ⓐ：你常常和朋友一起去學校跳舞嗎？
<small>cháng cháng　péng yǒu　　　　　　tiào wǔ</small>

LEARNING LOG

I can...	Excellent	Good	Fair	Needs Improvement
1 talk about my hobbies and ask about others' hobbies.	☐	☐	☐	☐
2 use "常常" appropriately in sentences to indicate the frequency of an action or event.	☐	☐	☐	☐
3 use "一邊……，一邊……" appropriately in sentences to indicate that two actions or events are occurring concurrently.	☐	☐	☐	☐
4 recognize the different forms of pronunciation of "好", "便", and "得".	☐	☐	☐	☐
5 write "唱", "歌", "朋", "友", and "常".	☐	☐	☐	☐

電視節目
Television Programs

My Goals

1 Talk about my favorite television programs
2 Ask about others' favorite television programs
3 Express the sequence of occurrence between two actions or events
4 Recognize some homophones (characters sharing the same pronunciation but have different meanings)
5 Become familiar with vocabulary associated with televiaion programs

diàn shì   jī
電視（機）

jié mù biǎo
節 目 表

xīn wén
新 聞

kǎ tōng
卡 通

diàn yǐng
電 影

lián xù jù
連 續 劇
(soap opera, drama series)

Play It

1 In small groups, discuss and come up with a list of shows that fall under the categories of television programs above.

2 Send a representative up front to present the list of shows your group has compiled.

3 The teacher will then write down the categories as headings on the board.

4 As a group, send another representative to stand in front of the board. The teacher will randomly name a television show. The representatives in front decide which category the show belongs to and try to be the first to tap the accurate heading on the board. The fastest group wins.

New Words

diàn shì jī	jié mù biǎo	xīn wén	kǎ tōng	diàn yǐng
電視（機）television	節目表 program schedule	新聞 news	卡通 cartoon	電影 movie

Let's CHANT Go300

dǎ kāi diàn shì jié mù
打開電視節目多，

xīn wén kǎ tōng jiā diàn yǐng
新聞卡通加電影，

yīng wén　　　　　xuǎn
英文中文自己選，

　　　　　jiǔ
可是不要看太久。

New Words

dǎ kāi 打開 turn on	jié mù 節目 program	jiā 加 and; add
yīng wén 英文 the English language	xuǎn 選 choose	jiǔ 久 long

很久
（jiǔ）

我找了很久，還是找不到圖書館。

弟弟選了很久，還是選不到想看的電影。

小貴學了很久，英文還是說不好。

小明寫了很久，作業還是寫不完。

TIP

"很……" is an objective expression specifying the degree to which the following adjective applies. "太……" is a subjective expression, suggesting that the degree of the adjective that follows is much greater than desired.

太久
（jiǔ）

電視不要看得太久。

弟弟電視看得太久了，所以作業還沒寫完。

小明打球打得太久了，所以還沒回家吃晚飯。

| 你 | 看哪個節目， | 我 | 就 | 看哪個節目。 |

jié mù ... *jié mù*

他看什麼電影，我就看什麼電影。 (*diàn yǐng* ... *diàn yǐng*)

同學買哪本書，他就買哪本書。

哥哥喝哪種果汁，妹妹就喝哪種果汁。 (*zhǒng* ... *zhǒng*)

同學選什麼課，我就選什麼課。 (*xuǎn* ... *xuǎn*)

TIP
This is a sentence structure where the second clause replicates the first clause. The question tag (什麼,哪個……) does not have any interrogative function and varies according to the noun following it.

| 看完電影， | 再 | 去圖書館。 |

diàn yǐng

吃完飯，再喝果汁。

寫完作業，再看電視。 (*diàn shì*)

跳完舞，再吃飯。

TIP
In these examples, "再" means "then" to express the sequence of two events. The event that occurs later is positioned after the word "再".

New Words

zhǒng
種 kind, type

Go300

WANT TO LEARN MORE?

Check out the Text > Sentence Pattern section in the Go300 CD.

Find a partner and practice the following dialogues.

Task 1

Ⓐ：你想看什麼電視節目？

Ⓑ：你看哪個節目，我就看哪個節目。

Ⓐ：我想看電影。

Ⓑ：你想看中文電影還是英文電影？

Ⓐ：我想看＿＿＿＿＿＿＿＿＿＿＿。

Task 2

Ⓐ：我喜歡看卡通，有的卡通很好笑 (amusing)。

Ⓑ：我弟弟也喜歡看卡通。可是媽媽要弟弟做完功課，再看卡通。

Ⓐ：我媽媽也要我們做完功課，再看電視。上個星期，我們看電視看得太久了，媽媽很生氣。

Task 3

Ⓐ：我每天都看一個小時的電視新聞，
diàn shì xīn wén

你看不看新聞？
xīn wén

Ⓑ：我也常常看新聞。
xīn wén

Ⓐ：你什麼時候看新聞？
xīn wén

Ⓑ：我吃完晚飯就會看新聞。
xīn wén

Task 4

Ⓐ：你常常看電視嗎？
diàn shì

Ⓑ：_____。

Ⓐ：你什麼時候看電視？
diàn shì

Ⓑ：_____。

Ⓐ：你最喜歡看什麼電視節目？
diàn shì jié mù

Ⓑ：_____。

The following dialogues are adapted from the Text > Dialogue section in your  . Listen to the CD before reading the transcript on this page.

⭐Task 5

Ⓐ : 你喜歡看什麼節目(jié mù)？

Ⓑ : 我喜歡看卡通(kǎ tōng)，每天下午四點半都有卡通(kǎ tōng)。

⭐Task 6

Ⓐ : 你想看哪個節目(jié mù)？請你自己選(xuǎn)。

Ⓑ : 沒關係，你看哪個節目(jié mù)，我就看哪個節目(jié mù)。

⭐Task 7

Ⓐ : 你在家看中文電視(diàn shì)還是英文電視(yīng wén diàn shì)？

Ⓑ : 爺爺奶奶他們看中文的，我們看英文(yīng wén)的。

⭐Task 8

Ⓐ : 你看了今天的新聞(xīn wén)了嗎？

Ⓑ : 還沒有，有什麼大新聞(xīn wén)？

Any hot news?

Let's Learn CHARACTER

Due to the morphology and the way characters were formed in the Chinese language, homophones (characters with the same pronunciation) are very common. There may be fewer homophones in other languages which use the alphabetical system of writing and pronunciation. Hence, a foreign learner of Chinese may be prone to confusion if he cannot tell the difference between homophones. In the following, we look at some homophones we have learnt before. Study them and note the differences—although they are pronounced the same way, there are vast differences in their morphology and their meanings.

shì

是 → 不是

事 → 做事

市 → 市場
shì   diàn shì

視 → 電視

shū

書 → 一本書

輸 → 輸贏

TIP In Chinese, "書" and "輸" sound the same. Hence, it is considered bad luck by some Chinese to receive a book as a present because it is thought that the present might bring about a loss to the recipient.

Practice It

Which of the following characters share the same *pinyin*? Write down the *pinyin* and the characters in the spaces below.

久　文　辛　聞　名　辛

新　九　心　鐘　問　種

pinyin	*pinyin*	*pinyin*
characters	**characters**	**characters**

弟弟說，電視^{diàn shì}是他的學校，他可以天天上學，

不休息。因為天天都有不同又好看的電視節目^{diàn shì jié mù}。有

英文節目^{yīng wén jié mù}、中文節目^{jié mù}，可以學英文^{yīng wén}，也可以學中文。

天天在家看電視^{diàn shì}，媽媽不用接送，也不用教他，他

可以自己學，又方便又好玩。

　　你說，弟弟說得對不對？

Answer these questions in Chinese.

1　What does the author's brother say his school is?

2　Why does he say he could go to school every day?

3　What does "可以學英文，也可以學中文" mean?

4　Who does "自己" in the phrase "他可以自己學" refer to?

LESSON 9

 Text 2 Go300

Read the following text carefully.

bān

爸爸一下班回家，就打開電視看新聞；
dǎ kāi diàn shì xīn wén

哥哥一下課回家，就打開電視看球賽；
dǎ kāi diàn shì

姊姊一下課回家，就打開電視看電影；
dǎ kāi diàn shì diàn yǐng

弟弟一下課回家，就打開電視看卡通；
dǎ kāi diàn shì kǎ tōng

媽媽叫：「吃飯了。」沒有人回答。
jiào

Answer these questions in Chinese.

1 What television programs does the author's family enjoy?
Write them down in the table below.

爸爸	哥哥	姊姊	弟弟

2 What does the author's mother want everybody to do?

3 At the end of this passage, nobody responds to the author's mother. What do you think happens next?
Try writing an ending to this story before checking out the ending in the CD (Text > Reading: 2-1).

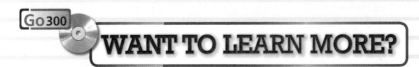

Go300

WANT TO LEARN MORE?

Check out the Text > Reading section in the Go300 CD.

Let's DO IT

1 Using the dialogue below, find out which category of television programs your classmates enjoy and how long they spend watching television every day. Record your findings in the table below.

2 Each group has to send a representative to the front to report the group's findings.

Ⓐ : 你最喜歡看什麼電視節目？
diàn shì jié mù

Ⓑ : 我最喜歡看電影。
diàn yǐng

Ⓐ : 你每天看多久 (how long) 電視？
duō jiǔ   diàn shì

Ⓑ : 我每天都看兩個小時的電視。
diàn shì

Name	Categories of television shows he or she enjoys	Duration spent on watching television every day

3. As an individual assignment, tally the findings of all the groups and find out the category most of your classmates enjoy. Write it down in the blank below.

Category enjoyed by most of my classmates: _____

今天天氣
The Weather Today

San Francisco
54-57°F/
12-14°C

Paris
59-79°F/
15-26°C

Taipei
75-90°F/
24-32°C

Cairo
75-100°F/
24-38°C

Sydney
48-64°F/
9-18°C

Rio De Janeiro
55-72°F/
13-22°C

My Goals

1 Describe the weather
2 Describe feelings of hot and cold
3 Illustrate in my sentences that an action is ongoing, or that two actions are occurring concurrently
4 Use the semicolon " ； " appropriately
5 Become familiar with vocabulary associated with the weather

Get Started

tài yáng
太陽

guā fēng
颱風

Play It

Charades: Send representatives from each group one by one to the teacher for a word or phrase. The representative has to act out the word or phrase and the rest of the class will try to figure it out. The group that guesses it first wins.

yáng guāng
陽光

xià yǔ
下雨

wū yún
烏雲
(dark clouds)

rè
熱

qíng tiān
晴天

yǔ tiān
雨天
(rainy day)

yīn tiān
陰天

lěng
冷

New Words

tài yáng 太陽 sun	yáng guāng 陽光 sunshine	qíng tiān 晴天 sunny day	guā fēng 颱風 wind blowing
xià yǔ 下雨 rain	yīn tiān 陰天 cloudy day; overcast day	rè 熱 hot	lěng 冷 cold

花，喜歡陽光，看著陽光笑；
yáng guāng *zhe yáng guāng xiào*

草，喜歡下雨，張著嘴喝水；
xià yǔ *zhāng zhe*

樹，喜歡颱風，唱著歌跳舞。
shù *guā fēng* *zhe*

 Think About It

Some people are cheered up by sunny days while rainy days depress them. Yet others are heartened by rainy days. What kind of weather do you like? Are your moods influenced by weather changes?

New Words

著 (an adverbial particle)	笑 laugh	張著 open	樹 tree
zhe	*xiào*	*zhāng zhe*	*shù*

Let's Learn GRAMMAR

著

哥哥唱著歌，妹妹跳著舞，

大家玩得很開心。

弟弟張著嘴想唱歌，可是他不會唱。

> There are two meanings to "著". Where it means the simultaneity of two actions, it has the same meaning as suggested in the sentence structure "一邊……，一邊……".
> For example, "姑姑聽著音樂跳舞。" means the same as "姑姑一邊聽音樂，一邊跳舞。".

> "著" in this instance indicates that an action is still on-going.

姑姑聽著音樂跳舞。

> "著" in this instance indicates that two actions are happening simultaneously: listening to music and dancing at the same time.

老師看著我說：「明天不要忘了交作業。」

qíng tiān   zhe yáng guāng xiào
爸爸喜歡晴天，他看著陽光笑。

……怎麼樣？

今天天氣怎麼樣？

他的心情怎麼樣？

你昨天看的電影怎麼樣？

這個星期日去看球賽怎麼樣？

> Here, "怎麼樣？" is used to ask somebody about a situation or for his opinion.

會

A：明天會很熱(rè)嗎？

B：我想明天會很熱(rè)。

A：明天你會很忙嗎？

B：明天我又要打球，又要參加樂隊，我會很忙。

TIP "會 + Adjective" indicates the possibility of a condition or situation.

"會 + Verb" indicates the capability of a person, often through some training or practice.

For example:

- 妹妹會唱歌。
- 弟弟會跳舞。

明天天氣好，	我們	就	去打球。

颳風(guā fēng)或(huò) (or) 下雨(xià yǔ)，我就不去看電影。

沒事做，我就會去打球。

有地圖(dì tú) (map)，我就找得到圖書館。

TIP These are hypothetical sentences which contain two clauses each. The clause which is led by "就" introduces the outcome that will follow only after the conditions in the preceding clause are met. The hypothetical tag "如果" or "要是 (if)" is omitted at the beginning of the sentences.

Go300 WANT TO LEARN MORE?

Check out the Text > Sentence Pattern section in the Go300 CD.

Find a partner and practice the following dialogues.

⭐ Task 1

Ⓐ ： 我每天都看電視新聞。 *xīn wén*

Ⓑ ： 你為什麼每天看新聞？

Ⓐ ： 看新聞可以知道 *zhī dào* (know) 很多不同的事 *tóng shì* ，
還可以知道 *zhī dào* 明天的天氣。

Ⓑ ： 明天有棒球比賽，會下雨嗎？ *xià yǔ*

Ⓐ ： 你看新聞就知道了。 *zhī dào*

⭐ Task 2

Ⓐ ： 今天外面冷不冷？ *wài miàn lěng lěng*

Ⓑ ： 今天天氣很好，外面不冷也不熱。 *wài miàn lěng rè*

Ⓐ ： 下午你有事嗎？你想不想去打球？

Ⓑ ： 下午我沒事。你想打什麼球？

Ⓐ ： 我們去打棒球怎麼樣？

Ⓑ ： 好，我喜歡打棒球。

New Words

wài miàn
外面 outside

Task 3

A： 你喜歡晴天還是雨天？
　　　　　qíng tiān　　　　　yǔ tiān

B： 我喜歡晴天，晴天我可以
　　　　qíng tiān　 qíng tiān

在草地上看書。你也喜歡

晴天嗎？
qíng tiān

A： 晴天、雨天我都喜歡。
　 qíng tiān　　yǔ tiān

我們一起去散步，好不好？
　　　　　　　sàn bù

B： 現在外面下著雨，我不想去。等一等，
　　 wài miàn xià zhe yǔ　　　　　　děng　 děng

不下雨了，我就和你一起去散步。
xià yǔ

Task 4

A： 春天、夏天、秋天和冬天，我最喜歡夏天。
　　　　　　　 qiū tiān

B： 我不喜歡夏天，因為夏天太熱了。
　　　　　　　　　　　　　 rè

C： 我最喜歡冬天。冬天天氣冷，會下雪。
　　　　　　　　　　　　 lěng

我喜歡玩雪球(snow ball)。
　　　 xuě qiú

D： 我最喜歡 春天，因為春天到了要種

花。

今天天氣　117

Task 5

Complete the dialogues below according to the pictures. When you have done that, listen to the Text >

Dialogue Section in your [Go 300] to compare your answers.

 1

A　明天天氣怎麼樣？

B　明天晴天。

 2

A　你明天會不會來
　　打球？

B　我不來，因為兩天。

 3

A　明天冷不冷？
　　　lěng　　lěng

B　不冷

4

A　明天會很熱嗎？
　　　　　rè

B　很熱

118　今天天氣

Let's Learn PUNCTUATION

；

fēn hào
分號
(semicolon)

The semicolon is often used between two semantically-connected sentences that either parallel or contrast each other. The semicolon is also commonly used at the end of a multi-clausal sentence to sum up the content of the entire sentence.

yáng guāng zhe yáng guāng xiào xià yǔ zhāng zhe
花，喜歡陽光，看著陽光笑；草，喜歡下雨，張著嘴喝水。

tài yáng xià yǔ
明天出太陽，我們就去球場打球；下雨，我們就在家裡玩遊戲。

xià yǔ shù yǔ shù guā fēng shù fēng shù
下雨，樹很開心，雨和樹一起玩遊戲；颳風，樹很開心，風和樹一起跳舞。

我有眼睛可以看，我有耳朵可以聽，我有手可以做事；這就是幸福。

Practice It

Fill in the blanks with the correct punctuation marks.

1. 張開眼睛，可以看；張開嘴，可以問問題。
2. 你姓張，他姓張，我也姓張；我們的姓都一樣。
3. yáng guāng qíng tiān wū yún yīn tiān xià yǔ yǔ tiān
有陽光，是晴天，有烏雲；是陰天，下雨了；是雨天。

Read the following text carefully.

爸爸開車送我去學校，他開著^{zhe}車，我唱著^{zhe}歌，

他笑著^{xiào zhe}問我：「喜歡上學嗎？」

我笑著^{xiào zhe}回答：「喜歡上學，我喜歡我的老師，

喜歡我的同學，也喜歡學校的活動。」

我笑著^{xiào zhe}問爸爸：「喜歡上班嗎？」

爸爸也笑著^{xiào zhe}回答：「喜歡上班，上班有事做，

上班有錢賺。」

爸爸笑著^{xiào zhe}說，我笑著^{xiào zhe}聽，我們一起唱歌，真是

開心的一天。

Answer these questions in Chinese.

1　Where does the above conversation take place? Besides talking, what else are the author and his father doing?

2　Do you think the author and his father are in a good mood? Why?

3　Does the author like to go to school? Why?

WANT TO LEARN MORE?

Check out the Text > Reading section in the Go300 CD.

Text 2

Read the following text carefully.

風*和太陽常常吵架。

風一邊吹*著，一邊說：「我是最強*的。」太陽

聽了很不開心，太陽想：「我才*是最強的。」風對

太陽說：「我們來比賽，怎麼樣？」太陽說：「太好

了！你看，地上有一個穿著大衣*的人，我

們來比一比，看誰能脫掉*他的大衣。」

風用力*吹著，吹了很久很久，還是沒有用。太

陽出來了，地上的人看著太陽說：「今天的太陽真

大，天氣真熱。」說完，就脫掉大衣了。

*吹 blow   *風 wind   *強 strong   *才 only (used for intensifying the tone)
*大衣 coat   *脫掉 take off   *用力 to exert (strength, force)

Answer these questions in Chinese.

1 What are the wind and the sun arguing about?

2 What do the wind and the sun do respectively to get the passerby to take off his coat?

3 Who is the winner in the end?

Weather Report

NEW YORK

1 Students will be divided into small groups. Each group will be in charge of finding out the weather forecast of a designated city for the coming week (as illustrated in the diagram above).

2 Create computer presentation slides or posters based on your findings. In a group, present the weather forecast to your class in the manner of a newscaster. Your report should include the following information:
   (1) Name of city
   (2) Dates of the forecast
   (3) Number of clear and cloudy days in the week; number of days of rain or snow in the week
   (4) The hottest and coldest days in the week

3 Students will vote for the group with the most comprehensive report, as well as the group which displays the most creativity in its preparation and presentation.

LEARNING LOG

I can...	Excellent	Good	Fair	Needs Improvement
1 talk about daily weather conditions in Chinese.	☐	☐	☐	☐
2 describe feelings of hot and cold according to how I feel.	☐	☐	☐	☐
3 use "著" to illustrate that an action is ongoing, or to describe two actions that are occurring concurrently.	☐	☐	☐	☐
4 use the semicolon (；) between two parallel or contrasting sentences.	☐	☐	☐	☐
5 write "陽", "著", "笑", "風", and "雨".	☐	☐	☐	☐

Vocabulary Index

Words indicated with an asterisk (*) are supplementary vocabulary from each lesson. They are included to supplement students' vocabulary and enhance their oral proficiency.

Pinyin	Bopomofo	Traditional Character	English	Simplified Character	Lesson
A					
ài hào	ㄞˋ ㄏㄠˋ	愛好	hobby	愛好	L8
B					
bàng qiú	ㄅㄤˋ ㄑㄧㄡˊ	棒球	baseball		L7
bào gào	ㄅㄠˋ ㄍㄠˋ	報告*	report	报告	L3
bí shuǐ	ㄅㄧˊ ㄕㄨㄟˇ	鼻水	mucus		L4
bǐ	ㄅㄧˇ	比	compare		L7
bǐ sài	ㄅㄧˇ ㄙㄞˋ	比賽	contest	比赛	L7
biǎo dì	ㄅㄧㄠˇ ㄉㄧˋ	表弟	younger cousin (male, both paternal and maternal)		L1
biǎo gē	ㄅㄧㄠˇ ㄍㄜ	表哥	older cousin (male, both paternal and maternal)		L1
biǎo jiě	ㄅㄧㄠˇ ㄐㄧㄝˇ	表姊	older cousin (female, both paternal and maternal)	表姐	L1
biǎo mèi	ㄅㄧㄠˇ ㄇㄟˋ	表妹	younger cousin (female, both paternal and maternal)		L1
bìng rén	ㄅㄧㄥˋ ㄖㄣˊ	病人*	patient		L4
bó bo	ㄅㄛˊ ㄅㄛ·	伯伯	uncle (father's older brother)		L1
bó mǔ	ㄅㄛˊ ㄇㄨˇ	伯母*	aunt (wife of father's older brother)		L1
C					
cān jiā	ㄘㄢ ㄐㄧㄚ	參加	join; participate in	参加	L2
cháng cháng	ㄔㄤˊ ㄔㄤˊ	常常	often		L8
chǎng	ㄔㄤˇ	場	(a measure word used for a contest)	场	L7
chàng gē	ㄔㄤˋ ㄍㄜ	唱歌	sing a song		L8
chǎo jià	ㄔㄠˇ ㄐㄧㄚˋ	吵架	quarrel		L6
chéng jī	ㄔㄥˊ ㄐㄧ	成績	grades	成绩	L3
chéng jī dān	ㄔㄥˊ ㄐㄧ ㄉㄢ	成績單*	school report card	成绩单	L3
chī yào	ㄔ ㄧㄠˋ	吃藥*	take medicine	吃药	L4
chū lái	ㄔㄨ ㄌㄞˊ	出來	come out	出来	L4
chū qù	ㄔㄨ ㄑㄩˋ	出去	go out		L4
cì	ㄘˋ	次	time; instance		L8

D

Pinyin	Zhuyin	Traditional	English	Simplified	Lesson
dǎ jià	ㄉㄚˇ ㄐㄧㄚˋ	打架	fight		L6
dǎ kāi	ㄉㄚˇ ㄎㄞ	打開	turn on	打开	L9
dà kǎo	ㄉㄚˋ ㄎㄠˇ	大考	final examination		L3
dài	ㄉㄞˋ	帶	bring	带	L6
de	ㄉㄜ・	得	(a particle used after a verb or an adjective to express possibility or capability)		L3
děi	ㄉㄟˇ	得	have to		L2
diàn shì (jī)	ㄉㄧㄢˋ ㄕˋ (ㄐㄧ)	電視(機)	television	电视(机)	L9
diàn yǐng	ㄉㄧㄢˋ ㄧㄥˇ	電影	movie	电影	L9
dù zi tòng	ㄉㄨˋ ㄗ・ ㄊㄨㄥˋ	肚子痛*	stomachache		L4
…duì	……ㄉㄨㄟˋ	……隊	team …	……队	L7
duì miàn	ㄉㄨㄟˋ ㄇㄧㄢˋ	對面	opposite	对面	L5

E

Pinyin	Zhuyin	Traditional	English	Simplified	Lesson
ér zi	ㄦˊ ㄗ・	兒子	son	儿子	L1

F

Pinyin	Zhuyin	Traditional	English	Simplified	Lesson
fā shāo	ㄈㄚ ㄕㄠ	發燒*	fever	发烧	L4
fàn guǎn	ㄈㄢˋ ㄍㄨㄢˇ	飯館	restaurant	饭馆	L5
fāng biàn	ㄈㄤ ㄅㄧㄢˋ	方便	convenient		L5
fēn	ㄈㄣ	分	score		L7
fù jìn	ㄈㄨˋ ㄐㄧㄣˋ	附近	nearby		L5

G

Pinyin	Zhuyin	Traditional	English	Simplified	Lesson
gěi	ㄍㄟˇ	給	give	给	L2
gōng yuán	ㄍㄨㄥ ㄩㄢˊ	公園*	park	公园	L5
gū gu	ㄍㄨ ㄍㄨ・	姑姑	aunt (father's sister)		L1
gū zhàng	ㄍㄨ ㄓㄤˋ	姑丈*	uncle (husband of father's sister)		L1
guā fēng	ㄍㄨㄚ ㄈㄥ	颱風	wind blowing	刮风	L10

H

Pinyin	Zhuyin	Traditional	English	Simplified	Lesson
hài pà	ㄏㄞˋ ㄆㄚˋ	害怕*	scared		L6
hē shuǐ	ㄏㄜ ㄕㄨㄟˇ	喝水*	drink water		L4
hé chàng tuán	ㄏㄜˊ ㄔㄤˋ ㄊㄨㄢˊ	合唱團*	choir	合唱团	L2
hù shì	ㄏㄨˋ ㄕˋ	護士*	nurse	护士	L4
huà huà	ㄏㄨㄚˋ ㄏㄨㄚˋ	畫畫*	paint	画画	L8

huài	ㄏㄨㄞˋ	壞	bad	坏	L3
huí jiā	ㄏㄨㄟˊ ㄐㄧㄚ	回家	go home		L2

J

jiā	ㄐㄧㄚ	加	and; add		L9
jiāo	ㄐㄧㄠ	交	hand in		L3
jié mù	ㄐㄧㄝˊ ㄇㄨˋ	節目	program	节目	L9
jié mù biǎo	ㄐㄧㄝˊ ㄇㄨˋ ㄅㄧㄠˇ	節目表	program schedule	节目表	L9
jìn	ㄐㄧㄣˋ	近	close, near		L5
jǐn zhāng	ㄐㄧㄣˇ ㄓㄤ	緊張	nervous	紧张	L7
jīng cǎi	ㄐㄧㄥ ㄘㄞˇ	精彩	outstanding, fantastic		L7
jiǔ	ㄐㄧㄡˇ	久	long		L9
jiù jiu	ㄐㄧㄡˋ ㄐㄧㄡ˙	舅舅	uncle (mother's brother)		L1
jiù mā	ㄐㄧㄡˋ ㄇㄚ	舅媽*	aunt (wife of mother's brother)	舅妈	L1

K

kǎ tōng	ㄎㄚˇ ㄊㄨㄥ	卡通	cartoon		L9
kāi xīn	ㄎㄞ ㄒㄧㄣ	開心	happy	开心	L6
kàn bìng	ㄎㄢˋ ㄅㄧㄥˋ	看病	see a doctor		L5
kàn diàn yǐng	ㄎㄢˋ ㄉㄧㄢˋ ㄧㄥˇ	看電影*	watch a movie	看电影	L8
kǎo	ㄎㄠˇ	考	take an exam		L3
kǎo juàn	ㄎㄠˇ ㄐㄩㄢˋ	考卷*	test paper		L3
kǎo shì	ㄎㄠˇ ㄕˋ	考試*	examination	考试	L3
ké	ㄎㄜˊ	咳	cough		L4
ké sòu	ㄎㄜˊ ㄙㄡˋ	咳嗽	cough		L4
kě shì	ㄎㄜˇ ㄕˋ	可是	but, however		L2
kè wài huó dòng	ㄎㄜˋ ㄨㄞˋ ㄏㄨㄛˊ ㄉㄨㄥˋ	課外活動	extra-curricular activity	课外活动	L2
kū	ㄎㄨ	哭*	cry		L6

L

lā lā duì	ㄌㄚ ㄌㄚ ㄉㄨㄟˋ	啦啦隊*	cheerleading	拉拉队	L2
lán qiú	ㄌㄢˊ ㄑㄧㄡˊ	籃球	basketball	篮球	L7
lěng	ㄌㄥˇ	冷	cold		L10
lí	ㄌㄧˊ	離	be away from	离	L5
lián xù jù	ㄌㄧㄢˊ ㄒㄩˋ ㄐㄩˋ	連續劇*	soap opera, drama series	连续剧	L9
liáo tiān	ㄌㄧㄠˊ ㄊㄧㄢ	聊天*	chat		L8

liú	ㄌㄧㄡˊ	流	flow	流		L4
liú bí shuǐ	ㄌㄧㄡˊ ㄅㄧˊ ㄕㄨㄟˇ	流鼻水	running nose	流鼻水		L4
M						
mà rén	ㄇㄚˋ ㄖㄣˊ	罵人	scold	骂人		L6
mǎi cài	ㄇㄞˇ ㄘㄞˋ	買菜	buy vegetables or groceries	买菜		L5
měi cì	ㄇㄟˇ ㄘˋ	每次	every time			L8
měi lì	ㄇㄟˇ ㄌㄧˋ	美麗	beautiful	美丽		L6
měi shì zú qiú	ㄇㄟˇ ㄕˋ ㄗㄨˊ ㄑㄧㄡˊ	美式足球*	American Football			L7
N						
nǎi nai	ㄋㄞˇ ㄋㄞ·	奶奶	grandmother (paternal)			L1
nán	ㄋㄢˊ	男	male			L1
nán guò	ㄋㄢˊ ㄍㄨㄛˋ	難過	miserable (L4) / sad (L6)	难过		L4/L6
nán kàn	ㄋㄢˊ ㄎㄢˋ	難看	terrible, ugly	难看		L6
nǚ ér	ㄋㄩˇ ㄦˊ	女兒	daughter	女儿		L1
P						
pǎo bù	ㄆㄠˇ ㄅㄨˋ	跑步	run, jog			L8
péng yǒu	ㄆㄥˊ ㄧㄡˇ	朋友	friend			L8
piào	ㄆㄧㄠˋ	票	ticket			L7
pīng pāng qiú	ㄆㄧㄥ ㄆㄤ ㄑㄧㄡˊ	乒乓球	table tennis			L7
Q						
qí yì shè	ㄑㄧˊ ㄧˋ ㄕㄜˋ	棋藝社*	chess club	棋艺社		L2
qíng tiān	ㄑㄧㄥˊ ㄊㄧㄢ	晴天	sunny day			L10
qiú chǎng	ㄑㄧㄡˊ ㄔㄤˇ	球場	court for ball games (basketball, tennis, etc.)	球场		L5
qiú duì	ㄑㄧㄡˊ ㄉㄨㄟˋ	球隊	ball team	球队		L2
qiú sài	ㄑㄧㄡˊ ㄙㄞˋ	球賽	ball game	球赛		L7
R						
rè	ㄖㄜˋ	熱	hot	热		L10
S						
shāng diàn	ㄕㄤ ㄉㄧㄢˋ	商店*	store			L5
shàng kè	ㄕㄤˋ ㄎㄜˋ	上課	go to class	上课		L2
shěn shen	ㄕㄣˇ ㄕㄣ·	嬸嬸*	aunt (wife of father's younger brother)	婶婶		L1
shēng bìng	ㄕㄥ ㄅㄧㄥˋ	生病	sick			L4

shēng qì	ㄕㄥ ㄑㄧˋ	生氣	angry	生气	L6
shí hòu	ㄕˊ ㄏㄡˋ	時候	time	时候	L3
shì chǎng	ㄕˋ ㄔㄤˇ	市場	market	市场	L5
shū	ㄕㄨ	輸	lose	输	L7
shū fǎ	ㄕㄨ ㄈㄚˇ	書法*	calligraphy	书法	L8
shú shu	ㄕㄨˊ ㄕㄨ˙	叔叔	uncle (father's younger brother)		L1
shù	ㄕㄨˋ	樹	tree	树	L10
shuǐ	ㄕㄨㄟˇ	水	water		L4
sòng	ㄙㄨㄥˋ	送	give (as a present)		L2
sūn nǚ	ㄙㄨㄣ ㄋㄩˇ	孫女	granddaughter (son's daughter)	孙女	L1
sūn zi	ㄙㄨㄣ ㄗ˙	孫子	grandson (son's son)	孙子	L1
suǒ yǐ	ㄙㄨㄛˇ ㄧˇ	所以	so	所以	L6

T

tài yáng	ㄊㄞˋ ㄧㄤˊ	太陽	sun	太阳	L10
táng gē	ㄊㄤˊ ㄍㄜ	堂哥	older cousin (male, paternal)		L1
táng mèi	ㄊㄤˊ ㄇㄟˋ	堂妹	younger cousin (female, paternal)		L1
tiào wǔ	ㄊㄧㄠˋ ㄨˇ	跳舞	dance		L8
tīng yīn yuè	ㄊㄧㄥ ㄧㄣ ㄩㄝˋ	聽音樂*	listen to music	听音乐	L8
tíng chē	ㄊㄧㄥˊ ㄔㄜ	停車	park (a vehicle)	停车	L5
tíng chē chǎng	ㄊㄧㄥˊ ㄔㄜ ㄔㄤˇ	停車場	parking lot	停车场	L5
tóng	ㄊㄨㄥˊ	同	the same		L1
tú shū guǎn	ㄊㄨˊ ㄕㄨ ㄍㄨㄢˇ	圖書館	library	图书馆	L5

W

wài gōng	ㄨㄞˋ ㄍㄨㄥ	外公	grandfather (maternal)		L1
wài miàn	ㄨㄞˋ ㄇㄧㄢˋ	外面	outside		L10
wài pó	ㄨㄞˋ ㄆㄛˊ	外婆	grandmother (maternal)		L1
wài sūn	ㄨㄞˋ ㄙㄨㄣ	外孫	grandson (daughter's son)	外孙	L1
wài sūn nǚ	ㄨㄞˋ ㄙㄨㄣ ㄋㄩˇ	外孫女	granddaughter (daugter's daughter)	外孙女	L1
wán	ㄨㄢˊ	完	finished		L3
wǎng qiú	ㄨㄤˇ ㄑㄧㄡˊ	網球*	tennis	网球	L7
wèi shén me	ㄨㄟˋ ㄕㄣˊ ㄇㄜ˙	為什麼	why, what for	为什么	L6
wū yún	ㄨ ㄩㄣˊ	烏雲*	dark clouds	乌云	L10

X

xǐ huān	ㄒㄧˇ ㄏㄨㄢ	喜歡	like	喜欢	L7
xià kè	ㄒㄧㄚˋ ㄎㄜˋ	下課	end of class	下课	L2
xià yǔ	ㄒㄧㄚˋ ㄩˇ	下雨	rain		L10
xiǎng	ㄒㄧㄤˇ	想	want		L2
xiàng	ㄒㄧㄤˋ	向	towards		L5
xiàng qián	ㄒㄧㄤˋ ㄑㄧㄢˊ	向前	forward		L5
xiàng qián zǒu	ㄒㄧㄤˋ ㄑㄧㄢˊ ㄗㄡˇ	向前走*	go ahead		L5
xiàng yòu zhuǎn	ㄒㄧㄤˋ ㄧㄡˋ ㄓㄨㄢˇ	向右轉*	turn right	向右转	L5
xiàng zuǒ zhuǎn	ㄒㄧㄤˋ ㄗㄨㄛˇ ㄓㄨㄢˇ	向左轉*	turn left	向左转	L5
xiǎo kǎo	ㄒㄧㄠˇ ㄎㄠˇ	小考	quiz		L3
xiǎo shí	ㄒㄧㄠˇ ㄕˊ	小時	hour	小时	L8
xiào	ㄒㄧㄠˋ	笑	laugh		L6*/L10
xiě zuò yè	ㄒㄧㄝˇ ㄗㄨㄛˋ ㄧㄝˋ	寫作業*	do homework	写作业	L3
xīn qíng	ㄒㄧㄣ ㄑㄧㄥˊ	心情	mood		L6
xīn wén	ㄒㄧㄣ ㄨㄣˊ	新聞	news	新闻	L9
xiū xí	ㄒㄧㄡ ㄒㄧˊ	休息	rest		L2
xuǎn	ㄒㄩㄢˇ	選	choose	选	L9
xué shēng huì	ㄒㄩㄝˊ ㄕㄥ ㄏㄨㄟˋ	學生會*	student union	学生会	L2
xué xiào	ㄒㄩㄝˊ ㄒㄧㄠˋ	學校	school	学校	L2

Y

yá tòng	ㄧㄚˊ ㄊㄨㄥˋ	牙痛*	toothache		L4
yáng guāng	ㄧㄤˊ ㄍㄨㄤ	陽光	sunshine	阳光	L10
yào	ㄧㄠˋ	藥	medicine	药	L4
yé ye	ㄧㄝˊ ㄧㄝ·	爺爺	grandfather (paternal)	爷爷	L1
yī shēng	ㄧ ㄕㄥ	醫生	doctor	医生	L4
yī yuàn	ㄧ ㄩㄢˋ	醫院	hospital	医院	L5
yí mā	ㄧˊ ㄇㄚ	姨媽	aunt (mother's sister)	姨妈	L1
yí zhàng	ㄧˊ ㄓㄤˋ	姨丈*	uncle (husband of mother's sister)		L1
yì jiā rén	ㄧˋ ㄐㄧㄚ ㄖㄣˊ	一家人	the whole family		L1
yì biān... yì biān...	ㄧˋ ㄅㄧㄢ……, ㄧˋ ㄅㄧㄢ……	一邊……, 一邊……	do the things at the same time	一边 , 一边	L8

yīn tiān	ㄧㄣ ㄊㄧㄢ	陰天	cloudy day; overcast day	阴天	L10
yīn wèi	ㄧㄣ ㄨㄟˋ	因為	because	因为	L6
yīn yuè	ㄧㄣ ㄩㄝˋ	音樂	music	音乐	L8
yīng wén	ㄧㄥ ㄨㄣˊ	英文	the English language	英文	L9
yíng	ㄧㄥˊ	贏	win	赢	L7
yòng xīn	ㄩㄥˋ ㄒㄧㄣ	用心	pay attention		L3
yóu jú	ㄧㄡˊ ㄐㄩˊ	郵局*	post office	邮局	L5
yòu zhuǎn	ㄧㄡˋ ㄓㄨㄢˇ	右轉	turn right	右转	L5
yǔ tiān	ㄩˇ ㄊㄧㄢ	雨天*	rainy day		L10
yuè duì	ㄩㄝˋ ㄉㄨㄟˋ	樂隊	music band	乐队	L2
yùn dòng	ㄩㄣˋ ㄉㄨㄥˋ	運動	exercise	运动	L7
Z					
zěn me	ㄗㄣˇ ㄇㄜ·	怎麼	how	怎么	L4
zhāng zhe	ㄓㄤ ㄓㄜ·	張著	open	张着	L10
zhe	ㄓㄜ·	著	(an adverbial particle)	着	L10
zhǒng	ㄓㄨㄥˇ	種	kind, type	种	L9
zhòng yào	ㄓㄨㄥˋ ㄧㄠˋ	重要	important		L3
zhù	ㄓㄨˋ	住	live		L5
zhuō qiú	ㄓㄨㄛ ㄑㄧㄡˊ	桌球	table tennis		L7
zì jǐ	ㄗˋ ㄐㄧˇ	自己	self		L6
zú qiú	ㄗㄨˊ ㄑㄧㄡˊ	足球*	soccer		L7
zuì	ㄗㄨㄟˋ	最	most		L3
zuǒ zhuǎn	ㄗㄨㄛˇ ㄓㄨㄢˇ	左轉	turn left	左转	L5
zuò yè	ㄗㄨㄛˋ ㄧㄝˋ	作業	homework	作业	L3